THE ORIGIN OF FREEMASONRY: THE 1717 THEORY EXPLODED

Published @ 2017 Trieste Publishing Pty Ltd

ISBN 9780649664184

The Origin of Freemasonry: The 1717 Theory Exploded by Chalmers I. Paton

Edited by Trieste Publishing Pty Ltd.
 Cover @ 2017

www.triestepublishing.com

CHALMERS I. PATON

THE ORIGIN OF FREEMASONRY: THE 1717 THEORY EXPLODED

 Trieste

The Origin of Freemasonry.

THE

ORIGIN OF FREEMASONRY:

THE 1717 THEORY EXPLODED.

BY

BROTHER CHALMERS I. PATON,

AUTHOR OF "FREEMASONRY IN RELATION TO CIVIL AUTHORITY AND THE FAMILY CIRCLE"
AND "FREEMASONRY AND ITS JURISPRUDENCE."

LONDON:

WILLIAM REEVES, 83, CHARING CROSS ROAD, W.C.

Printed by The New Temple Press, 17 Grant Road, Croydon.

PREFACE.

MANY worthy brethren have been offended on account
of the discredit done to the Masonic Order by the
assertion, which is now often and confidently made,
that the whole system of Freemasonry is of very
recent origin—some saying that it was invented by
Elias Ashmole and a few of his learned and ingenious
friends in the seventeenth century,—others, more
numerous, that it derives existence from the year 1717,
and was devised, promulgated, and palmed upon the
world by Dr Desaguliers, Dr Anderson, and others,
who then founded the Grand Lodge of England.
Some of these brethren have asked me, as a brother
believed to take a deep interest in every question of
this kind, and supposed to have opportunity for
investigation, to bestow a little attention upon this
subject—to inquire what grounds there are for the
Ashmole theory, and what for the 1717 theory—or if
they are not both utterly groundless. I have gladly
endeavoured to comply with their request, and hope
the result may be satisfactory to them. Whatever

they or others may think of my pamphlet, I feel convinced that the proof which it sets forth is sufficient,
and the argument conclusive, and this is all—or
almost all—that I care for in the matter. I have a
strong desire to see the honour of our Order maintained, and to contribute my own part in every
way possible to the maintaining of it; and I believe nothing can be more contrary to it than the
supposition that Freemasonry is of recent origin. For,
if it were so, it would be liable to be regarded not
merely as an invention of men of talent, which might
be good, but, of necessity, as an imposture, which in no
case can be imagined to be good. When we consider
how Freemasonry was presented to public notice in
England, after the foundation of the Grand Lodge in
1717, we must feel ourselves constrained either to
acknowledge that Dr Desaguliers, Dr Anderson, and
their coadjutors, were honest men doing a work which
they believed to be good, or to set them down as a
set of the most consummate rascals that ever imposed
upon mankind, and yet with no motive for their imposture. No motive has ever been assigned or suggested. The case is one which needs to be plainly
stated, and which the supporters of the 1717 theory
must meet in the plainest statement of it. To maintain the honour or excellence of Freemasonry, and at
the same time to maintain its base origin, is ridiculous.
Looking to the characters of Dr. Desaguliers and Dr.

Anderson, it seems impossible to doubt their thorough honesty and integrity. This of itself is a powerful argument; but another equally powerful is to be found in the character of the system which they did so much to promote in England and in the world—a system of high and pure morality. But I must not further anticipate, in the preface, the argument of the pamphlet itself, which I now respectfully commend to the attention of the members of the Masonic brotherhood.

ORIGIN OF FREEMASONRY.

THE 1717 THEORY EXPLODED.

IT has of late been asserted, with no small display of confidence, but without any display of evidence, that the present system of Freemasonry or what is called Speculative Masonry, had its origin in the year 1717, when the Grand Lodge of England was formed. The purpose of the present pamphlet is to submit this theory to examination.

The first thing which naturally occurs to the mind in considering this theory, is the perfectly arbitrary character of the assumption which is made. Why should it be assumed that Speculative Masonry originated in 1717? Why should not another date be fixed upon as readily as that which is assumed? In fact, we know that some of those who have recently opposed the notion of the great antiquity of Freemasonry, have assigned another date for its origin. They represent it as having been devised and framed into a System by the celebrated Elias Ashmole and others, about the middle of the seventeenth century, or about fifty years before 1717. All this it is proposed to consider in the following pages, that the baselessness of the one theory may be exhibited as well as that of the other. In the meantime, reference is merely made to what may be called the Seventeenth Century theory, as showing the difference of opinion or of conjecture which exists among those who assign to Speculative Masonry an entirely modern origin. If the one theory, however, were merely to be balanced against the

other, those who go back to the seventeenth century would
be found to have the advantage; for evidence of the existence of Speculative Freemasonry can easily be adduced from
the writings of Elias Ashmole himself. We shall see this as
we proceed. Meanwhile, it is only necessary to advert to the
fact, as showing how ungrounded the 1717 theory is. Evidence will be hereafter adduced to show that Speculative
Masonry existed not only before 1717, but before the time
of Ashmole.

The advocates of the 1717 theory found their chief
argument on the formation of the Grand Lodge of England
in that year. They tell us of Dr Desaguliers, Dr Anderson,
and others, as the framers or inventors of the new system.
There is no doubt that the present Grand Lodge of England
was founded in 1717. There is also no doubt that Dr
Desaguliers and Dr Anderson took part in founding it, nor
that to them we are greatly indebted for the high position
which Freemasonry then assumed, and which it has since
maintained in this country. That they also improved the
system is not to be denied. It is a system which has
undergone improvement since its beginning, and is capable
of indefinite improvement. But that Dr Desaguliers and
Dr Anderson invented it,—that they palmed it upon the
world as an ancient institution, whilst they knew it to be a
mere novelty of their own framing,—is a supposition utterly
inconsistent with the characters of the men, even if there were
nothing in the facts of history to refute it. Dr Desaguliers, a
Frenchman, was carried from his native country in childhood
by his parents, Huguenot refugees, and, being educated in
England, spent his life there, became thoroughly naturalised,
writing his works in English, and not in the language of his
native country. He was eminent in Natural Philosophy and
Natural History, in both departments of science one of the
first men of his day; a voluminous author, whose works are
even now consulted by those who study the branches of
science to which he devoted himself. Dr Anderson, a Scots-
man, was a Presbyterian minister in London, of high repute
amongst his brethren, and of note also for his literary

attainments. Desaguliers was excelled, as a natural philosopher, perhaps by none of his contemporaries, except Sir
Isaac Newton and Halley. Anderson was, like him, a
man of high character, and in great esteem. These men,
it may safely be said, were not likely to frame a system of
imposture, and to employ their time in deceiving others
by so doing, even if they had a motive of advantage;
whereas no such motive is suggested by those who gratui-
tously attribute to them this conduct, and they are represented
as doing what they are said to have done in the foundation
of Speculative Freemasonry without any reason or motive
whatever. There can be nothing more improbable than this
theory. The most positive evidence must be demanded in
its support; and of such evidence nothing whatever has been
adduced.

Let it be observed, that this 1717 theory ascribes to men
of the highest character the invention of a system of mere
imposture. For whatever that system may be deemed in
itself,—and we may well refer to its nature as showing how
unlikely it is to have had such an origin,—yet if it was framed
and palmed upon the world by Desaguliers and others in
1717, it was nothing else than a system of imposture. It
was brought forward with pretensions which its framers
knew to be false, pretensions of high antiquity; whereas,
according to the 1717 theory, it had been newly invented
in their studies. Is this likely? or is it reasonable to ascribe
such conduct to honourable men, without even assigning
a probable motive for it? It is rather a wanton traducing
of characters which have always been held in high regard.
Surely the eminent men of former generations ought to be
safe now from such attacks upon their reputation.

It is assumed in the 1717 theory that the Masons in
England, Scotland, and other countries, were, until that
date, a mere guild of operatives, like other guilds which
existed. It is forgotten that the very art of Masonry
required, in its higher departments, the possession of attainments by no means requisite in any of the other ordinary
crafts. The mere builder or hewer of stone might be nothing

more than an operative mason ; but those who planned a
building and superintended its erection, must always have
been men of highly superior culture and intelligence.   It
is to them that we ascribe the origin of Freemasonry; and
it seems certainly not improbable, but in the highest degree
probable, that the craft has existed from very ancient times,
distinct from all other crafts, and peculiar in its organisation.   Those who date its origin from the building of
Solomon's Temple, may have no very positive evidence to
sustain their theory, but it is at least in this respect better
than the 1717 theory, that it has in it more natural probability, and cannot so easily be refuted.   We can trace a
strong resemblance to the modern system of Freemasonry
in the architectural *collegia* of the ancient Romans.   We
find a similar system prevailing in the middle ages in the
Steinmetzen of Germany.   Had these, it may be asked, no
connection with one another?   It appears more than probable that they had, and that from them we may trace the
origin of the Freemasonry now existing.   It may be that
there were great and important differences, yet the most
essential parts of the system might be the same, and
indeed, it appears that they were the same.   In maintaining the antiquity of Freemasonry, it is by no means
requisite to prove that the system of former ages was
precisely the same as the present.   If we find in it the
same essential characters, it is enough.   The Freemasonry
of most modern times has undergone change.   Improvements
have been introduced from one time to another, and are
being introduced at the present day.   This susceptibility of
improvement is one of the excellences of Freemasonry.   It
may be admitted, without hesitation, that the system
previously existing was much improved by Desaguliers,
Anderson, and others, about 1717.   It may be admitted,
also that, half a century before, it was much improved by
Elias Ashmole and his coadjutors.   But this leaves us still
to suppose that they found a system in existence, which
they regarded as valuable, and which therefore they sought
to improve.

MUCH stress is laid by those who maintain the very recent origin of Freemasonry on the merely recent use of the term *Freemason*. I am not prepared to say when it began to be used, or how it came into use, although I will give abundant proof of its being in use long before 1717. The question, however, is one merely for the student of language, and has nothing to do with that now under consideration. The old term is *Mason*, and not *Freemason;* and the old term is still the only one acknowledged in the craft, the use of the other being merely popular. We speak of *making a Mason*, not of *making a Freemason;* our lodges are called *Masonic Lodges*, we never term them *Freemasonic*. The argument derived from the use of this term *Freemason* is of no value whatever.

Nor is it of any consequence to show that the Masons of England, Scotland, and other countries, were, in some respects, a guild or operative craft, like other guilds. The real question is, Were they *merely* so, or did they hold a high position above all other guilds or crafts, in virtue of which they received privileges and dignities which these did not, and this because of high and noble purposes and attainments peculiar to themselves? Masonry is a subject with which, in its higher departments, men cannot deal without a cultivation of mind which is not required in any of the other pursuits that guilds have been formed to protect or to promote. The men who built Westminster Abbey, or the Abbey of Melrose, must needs have possessed attainments beyond most of their contemporaries, or indeed the most distinguished men of more recent times. Their works command an admiration which increases the more that they are contemplated. No doubt, many mere operative masons were employed, who knew little more than their work of hewing and building; but they were governed and directed by the men who planned these glorious buildings, and superintended the execution of their design. They belonged to the same craft, it may be admitted; but it cannot be admitted that the operatives alone formed the craft. On the contrary, it may be deemed certain that the men who designed these buildings, and superintended the erection of them, were in all things the leaders and rulers of the craft or guild, if it is to be so called. It took its character from them, and not from the mere operative masons, any more than from the labourers and hodmen.

On account of the peculiar nature of the masonic craft, and the purposes which it aimed at, it obtained the patronage and support of kings, princes, nobles, and eminent churchmen, who were glad to become connected with it, and to learn something of what it had to teach. If we look at the history of Masonry, we find some of the Saxon and early Norman kings of England mentioned as eminent patrons of the craft; and in the beginning of the reign of Edward I., A.D. 1272, we find the care of the masons in England to have been intrusted to Walter Giffard, Archbishop of York; Gilbert de Clare, Earl of Gloucester; and Ralph, Lord of Mount Heomer, the progenitor of the family of Montague, who superintended the completion of Westminster Abbey, which had been begun in 1220, during the minority of Henry III. (*Preston's Illustrations of Masonry*, pp. 135, 136). Are these historical records to be set aside as utterly fabulous, and the invention of a recent time? We must see some reason for adopting this opinion before we do adopt it, and no reason is yet forthcoming. We are also told that Edward III. was a distinguished patron of Masonry, and encourager of learning. He is said to have revised the ancient charges, and to have added to the old code of laws. He appointed five deputies to inspect the proceedings of the fraternity, and many great buildings were erected during his reign. Is all this to be set down as fabulous, because men adopt the theory of 1717? Or, are we to imagine that the Masonry of Edward III.'s time was essentially different from that of the eighteenth century and the present? There would need be some positive proof to assure us of this, which proof is absolutely awanting.

It is not necessary for our purpose to trace the history of Masonry in England,—to take particular notice of the Act of Parliament for abolishing the Society of Masons, or at least for preventing their assemblies and congregations, in the beginning of the reign of Henry VI., or their subsequent prosperity, through the favour of the Duke of Gloucester, the Protector of the kingdom, in a later period of Henry VI.'s minority. It is enough to allude to these recorded facts of their history, as showing that they were no mere common craft or guild, but held a high and peculiar position of their own. Sir Thomas Sackville was Grand Master of the Masons of England in the reign of Queen Elizabeth. The Grand Lodge then assembled in York. The Queen, being jealous of secret assemblies, sent an armed force to York to break up the Annual Grand Lodge; but Sir Thomas Sackville prudently initiated some of the officers, who then made a favourable report to the Queen, so that she countermanded her orders, and the meetings of the fraternity were ever afterwards held in peace. Such is the story told in our masonic histories. Is it likely, we would ask, that the whole story is a fable,—a mere lie invented in a subsequent age? If not, it affords us proof of the existence of a masonic body, not entirely composed of operative masons, long before the beginning of the eighteenth century.

We go on, however, with the history of Freemasonry. Sir Thomas Sackville is said to have resigned the office of Grand Master in 1567 in favour of Francis Russell, Earl of Bedford, and Sir Thomas Gresham, an eminent merchant. The Earl of Bedford became Grand Master of the Masons in the northern parts of England, and Sir Thomas Gresham in the south; but the general assemblies were still held at York as before, and to these all appeals were made. There is some obscurity as to this part of the history, and the relations of the lodges and Grand Masters in different parts

of the kingdom, which we cannot attempt to remove, nor is
it necessary for our present purpose. Those who maintain
the 1717 theory must hold it all to be a fable, but it
behoves them to show when and by whom this fable
was invented, or in some way to show that it is a fable.
In the meantime, no evidence to the contrary having
been adduced, we must hold it to be authentic history.
In like manner we deem it true, as is asserted in our
best masonic histories, that the celebrated architect Inigo
Jones was nominated Grand Master of England by
James I., and was succeeded by the Earl of Pembroke in
1618. We deem it needless to trace this history farther.
Enough has been stated to show how high a position the
masonic body held in England from a very early period
down to the days of modern civilisation. Now we turn to
Scotland, and without going back to the days when Melrose
Abbey and the Cathedral of Glasgow were built, we begin
with the historic statement that in the reign of James II.
the office of Grand Master was granted by the King to
William St Clair of Roslin, Earl of Orkney and Caithness,
one of the greatest nobles of the kingdom, and the founder
of the exquisitely beautiful chapel of · Roslin. The office
was made hereditary to his successors, Lairds of Roslin, and
was accordingly held by the St Clairs of Roslin till 1736,
when it was resigned by William St Clair of Roslin in order
to the formation of a Grand Lodge of Scotland, with the
right of electing its own Grand Master. The Earl of Orkney,
to whom the grant was made by James II., held his earldom, then dependent on the crown of Norway, and not of
Scotland, in virtue of his marriage with an heiress of the
former Earl of Orkney. James II. created him Earl of
Caithness, but the estates of Roslin were better than all his
other estates; and accordingly, as his successors, the St Clairs
of Roslin, afterwards maintained, he bestowed them by his
will on his eldest son, leaving to a younger son the earldom
of Caithness. The Caithness family have, however, always
disputed this, maintaining that the earldom of Caithness
was inherited by the eldest son. It is not necessary for us

to enter into this question. There is no doubt that, at that date, earldoms as well as lairdships were often disposed of by will without that absolute regard to primogeniture which the law now requires. Be this as it may, the inheritance of the Grand Mastership of Masons was connected with the possession of the Barony of Roslin, and was held by the St Clairs of Roslin for several generations. The original charter granting this office is not extant, having been destroyed by fire in the Castle of Roslin, with other charters of the family, as we learn from a charter granted evidently in the reign of James VI. of Scotland, and probably after his accession to the throne of England, although it is without date. A copy of this charter is to be found in the Advocates' Library of Edinburgh, in the MSS. compiled by Father Augustin Hay, a Roman Catholic priest, about the year 1700. The date of this charter is made certain, within a few years, by a subsequent charter, of which a copy is also preserved in the same volume in the Advocates' Library, and which repeats all that it contains, with considerable amplification. This charter bears the date 1630, in the reign of Charles I. In these charters, the Masons of Scotland declare that from age to age the Lairds of Roslin have been patrons and protectors of them and their privileges; and they refer to the fact that the ancient charters had been destroyed by fire, and express their desire that the St Clairs of Roslin should procure from the King the same jurisdiction over them which their predecessors had so long possessed. It seems impossible to interpret this as relating to the mere patronage of a guild or craft, which could imply no honour or advantage, but only trouble; still less is it possible to attach such a meaning to the words of the charter, when it says that the Lairds of Roslin would " lay out of their just right" if they were not acknowledged in their high dignity by the Masons of Scotland. We also find mention in the charter of 1630 " of the auld good skill and judgment which the said William St Clair, now of Roslin, has in our said craft and vocation." Such language would be merely ridiculous in reference to any

other craft or guild that ever existed in Scotland, and to'
any person in such position as the St Clairs of Roslin held.
As to that position, it may be enough to remark, that
although never elevated to the peerage,—which in those
days was a somewhat different thing from what it is now
esteemed,—they were frequently summoned to attend
Parliament, and took their place accordingly among the
representatives of the Scottish barons, although not elected
by their fellow-barons or lairds, but called to Parliament
by the sovereign, according to an exercise of royal pre-
rogative which fell into desuetude, and of which we have
perhaps the last example in their case.   It is to be remembered that in ancient times the distinction between the
greater and lesser barons, the *barones majores* and *barones
minores*, was not so great as it afterwards became; the
former were not exactly *peers*, nor the latter *commoners*, in
our present acceptation of these terms ; and the St Clairs
of Roslin, as among the most wealthy and powerful of the
barons, held a position which probably they would not have
exchanged for that of many a Scottish earl.

The question may here be asked,—and it is one to which
those who maintain that Masonry was a mere'common craft
or guild till the seventeenth or till the beginning of the
eighteenth century, are surely bound to find an answer,—
What other craft or guild was patronised in a similar manner,
or had at its head any of the great nobles either of England
or Scotland ?   Was there ever an Earl of Mar, or an Earl
of Murray, or an Earl of Buchan, or a laird of high distinction, or any person whatever of high distinction, appointed
by the sovereign, or appointed in any way to be at the head
of the tailors or the cordwainers, or any of the other merely
operative crafts?   Until this question is answered in the
affirmative, we must hold that there was a wide and essential difference between these crafts and that of the Masons,
not only in the nature of the work done by the mere operatives, but in the position which the craft held and the
honour of being connected with it.

THERE is another consideration which it seems proper to bring forward, as of itself sufficient to refute the 1717 theory; and it is to be borne in mind that the argument which it suggests is altogether distinct from, and independent of, any which has yet been used. If Desaguliers and others, in the beginning of the eighteenth century, in 1717, or any other year, invented and palmed upon their fellowmen the system which is now called Masonry or Freemasonry, pretending it to be of high antiquity, why did they make choice of the masonic craft as that to which to attach themselves and their new system? There must have been some reason for the choice. It may safely be said that when we seek a probable reason for it, we shall find it exactly such as will make it seem highly probable that they found in that craft a system already in existence, which attracted their admiration, and which they deemed worthy of being wrought out to greater perfection. On this supposition, all is simple and capable of easy explanation; but on any other, an explanation will be hard to find.

Again, let it be asked, how if Desaguliers, and one or two others along with him, invented the present system of Freemasonry about the year 1717, they found so many of their contemporaries willing to join them, to accept the new system, and to accept it as ancient? Here we have another argument not easily to be refuted in favour of an antiquity of Freemasonry at least greater than the date so arbitrarily assigned to it. If Desaguliers and his associates had been guilty of imposture, can it be conceived that they would have been thus successful? Would the imposture not at once have been detected and exposed? Now, so far was this from being the case, that when the Grand Lodge of England was founded in 1717, many noblemen of the highest rank, and many other persons of the greatest distinction, speedily joined it. Were they all utterly deluded, or did they join in a conspiracy to pass off upon mankind a newly-invented system as one of venerable antiquity? Neither supposition is easily made, but the advocates of the 1717 theory must take their choice of the one or the other. It may well be supposed that in putting forth their theory they have not considered this. But that this necessity is involved in the theory, it would not be easy for them to deny. It reduces their position to one of absolute absurdity.

It is proper that we should look a little more closely to the circumstances which attended the foundation of the Grand Lodge of England. Masonry, it is admitted by all who believe in its existence from a much more ancient period, was in a very low state in England and throughout the world in the end of the seventeenth and beginning of the eighteenth century. But Dr Desaguliers, Dr Anderson, and others, about the end of the year 1716 or the beginning of 1717, took steps for its revival. There were four Lodges of Masons in London, and, at the instigation of these brethren, the four Lodges met together at the Apple-Tree Tavern in Charles Street, Covent Garden, and having voted the oldest Master-mason then present into the chair, they constituted themselves a Grand Lodge, *pro tempore*, in due form, and forthwith revived the quarterly communications of the officers of the Lodges, resolved to hold the annual assembly and feast, and then to choose a Grand Master among themselves till they should have the honour of a noble brother at their head. Thus the original steps taken for the foundation of the Grand Lodge of England are stated, and there seems to be no reason to doubt the historic accuracy of the statement, which has never, indeed, that I am aware of, been called in question. Amongst our modern writers we find Findel contending for the modern origin of Freemasonry, and rejecting, with much show of research and learning, the idea of its high antiquity. Others have adopted the same views, and without any show of research or learning, reiterate their assertions, and express contempt for every opposing argument. They have taken for granted that the whole thing has been settled by those who have studied it before them: and now their chosen work is to assure the world of this, concerning which, if mere repetition of statement were of any value, no one would have any excuse for doubt. But what are we to think of the facts before us? We take them in relation merely to the 1717 theory, and without reference at present to the question of the origination of Freemasonry in the seventeenth century by Ashmole and others. Do they not plainly imply the existence of a system prior to 1717, upon which Desaguliers, Anderson, and their co-adjutors founded? What were these four Lodges, of the existence of which these pretended framers of modern Free-masonry took advantage? What were the other Lodges throughout England to which they addressed their letters, inviting them, as we are told they did, to send their repre-sentatives to the next meeting of the newly-formed Grand Lodge? Can the members of these four Lodges of Lon-don, and the members of all the other Lodges of England which they invited to concur with them, have been deluded into the belief that they had existed from some long anterior time, and drawn at once, without a dissentient voice, into the acceptance of a system of absolute novelty, pretended to be ancient? No more improbable supposition was ever placed before the minds of men.

On St John Baptist's Day, 24th June 1717, the brethren again met in London, and by a majority of votes elected Brother Anthony Sayer, Grand Master of Masons, and he being forthwith invested with the badges of office and power by the oldest Master, and installed, was duly congra-tulated by the assembly, who paid him homage. Captain Joseph Elliot and Mr Jacob Lamball were appointed Grand Wardens. But again we pause to ask how all this is to be reconciled with the notion of a mere new invention? Why, then, this recognition of the oldest Master Mason present as entitled to a high place? Whence this imme-diate investiture with the badges of office, and this appoint-ment of Wardens? Is it not evident that there were already existing rules to be observed, the existence of which implies a higher antiquity of the system?

We may say, with confidence, that the whole history of the steps taken in 1717 affords proof of the existence of a system of Masonry anterior to that date,—a system acknowledged to have been handed down from more early times? There is nothing in it which corresponds with the notion of a newly-invented system, but, on the contrary, it assumes the system to be already in existence.

Now, let us go a little farther back, and inquire if the system of Masonry or Freemasonry existed in the seventeenth century. The evidence of its existence then, if it can be produced, must be fatal to the 1717 theory; and leads us a step farther towards proving its high antiquity. Evidence of this kind can be produced in abundance. Reference has already been made to the theory which has been propounded, that modern or speculative Masonry was invented by Elias Ashmole and some of his literary associates, in the latter part of the seventeenth century. But how does this theory accord with facts? Ashmole says in his diary, " I was made a Freemason at Warrington, Lancashire, with Colonel Henry Mainwaring, of Kirthingham, in Cheshire, by Mr Richard Penket, the Warden, and the fellow-crafts, on the 16th of October 1646." Here it may be observed in passing, that we have an instance of the use of the term *Freemason* in the seventeenth century; although, for reasons already assigned, this may be deemed of little importance. It is of far more importance to inquire how such a man as Ashmole,—an eminent natural philosopher, chemist, and antiquary, and the founder of the noble museum at Oxford which bears his name,—ever thought of being *made a Mason*. With operative masonry he had nothing to do, and there must have been something in the Masonry of his time to induce him to take part in it. He continued to the end of his life a zealous member of the craft, and is known to have projected a work on the history of Masonry. Not only does all this forbid the idea that Freemasonry was invented in 1717, but it forbids the idea that it was invented by Ashmole himself. Another passage may be quoted from Ashmole's diary, as showing the state of things in the latter part of the seventeenth century. " On March the 10th, 1682," he says, " about 5 *hor. post merid.*, I received a summons to appear at a Lodge to be held next day at Mason Hall, in London, March 11, 1682. Accordingly I went, and about noon was admitted into the fellowship of Freemasons,—Sir William Wilson, knight, Captain Richard Borthwick. Mr William Woodman, Mr William Grey, Mr Samuel Taylor, and Mr William Wise. I was the senior fellow among them,—it being thirty-five years since I was admitted. There were present, besides myself, the fellows after named :—Mr Thomas Wise, Master of the Masons' Company this present year; Mr Thomas Shorthose, &c. We all dined at the Half-Moon Tavern, in Cheapside, at a noble dinner, prepared at the charge of the new-accepted Masons."'

Here again we have the term Freemason used in the seventeenth century. But, as has already been said, this is of little consequence, except, indeed, that it shows how hastily the supposed mere recent use of this term has been accepted as an argument against the antiquity of Freemasonry, and how little those are to be trusted who use such arguments. The evidence, however, afforded by this passage is conclusive as to the existence of masonic Lodges in 1682, *of which the members were not all mere operative masons.* Indeed, we may well suppose that no mere operative mason was present at the Lodge meeting which Ashmole mentions, but that all were gentlemen, such as those whom he names. He evidently appears to have felt honoured by his connection with the Lodge, and to have delighted in the society into which he was brought at its meetings. The idea of a mere operative craft, or a Lodge of mere operative masons, is out of the question. Thus, then, we have conclusive evidence that a system of Freemasonry existed many years before 1717, having those distinctive characters which belong to modern Freemasonry, and wholly different from a mere operative craft or guild.

Another important document of the end of the seventeenth century is the often-quoted letter of the celebrated John Locke to the Earl of Pembroke, concerning a MS.

in the Bodleian Library. It has not been alleged that this letter is a fabrication; and supposing it, as we seem entitled to suppose it, to be genuine, it affords incontestible evidence of the existence of speculative, as distinguished from mere operative masonry, at the date of its composition. It may be best to quote the letter itself.

"*6th May* 1696.

"My Lord,—I have at length, by the help of Mr Colins, procured a copy of that MS. in the Bodleian Library which you were so curious to see; and, in obedience to your Lordship's commands, I herewith send it to you. Most of the notes annexed to it are what I made yesterday for the reading of my Lady Masham, who is become so fond of Masonry as to say that she now more than ever wishes herself a man, that she might be capable of admission into the fraternity.

"The MS. of which this is a copy appears to be about a hundred and sixty years old; yet (as your Lordship will observe by the title) it is itself a copy of one yet more ancient by about a hundred years,—for the original is said to have been in the handwriting of King Henry VI. When that prince had it, is at present an uncertainty; but it seems to me to be an examination (taken perhaps before the King) of some one of the brotherhood of Masons,—among whom he entered himself, as it is said, when he came out of his minority, and thenceforth put a stop to the persecution that had been raised against them. But I must not detain your Lordship longer by my preface from the thing itself."

Can any evidence be more conclusive than that afforded by this letter of the existence of a fraternity of Masons in England, practising speculative Masonry as well as operative, in the end of the seventeenth century, regarded then as ancient, and as having enjoyed the favour of the great in former days? There must have been something very peculiar about the character of that fraternity, as to which "my Lady Masham" wished that she were a man in order that she might be capable of admission into it. It must have been something very different from an ordinary guild.

As to the MS. in the Bodleian Library itself, it also affords important evidence of the existence and nature of Masonry

B

long before the end of the seventeenth century. We may take it for granted that the MS. was then, as Locke says, about a hundred and sixty years old. We need not assume that the original from which it was copied was in the handwriting of King Henry VI., and yet probably it carries us back to about the time of his reign, the middle of the fifteenth century. It is not necessary for our present argument, however, to be particular about a hundred years or so in the date. It is enough for us to consider the document as of a date long anterior to the beginning of the eighteenth century—probably at least two hundred years, and perhaps more than two hundred and fifty years before that date. What, then, is the evidence which it affords? It proves beyond controversy that there existed in England a fraternity of masons, professing to be of very ancient origin. Their origin in England is referred to "Peter Gower, a Grecian," whose name Locke in a note suggests to be a corruption of Pythagoras. "Peter Gower," it is said, "whenne he journeydde to lernne, was ffyrste made, and anonne techedde; evenne so should all others beyn recht. Natheless Maconnes haue the always yn everyche time from tyme to tyme communycatedde to mankynde soche of her secrettes as generallyche myghte be usefulle, they haueth keped backe soche allein as shulde be harmefulle yff they comed yn euill haundes, oder soche as ne myghte be holpynge withouten the techynges to be joined herwythe in the lodge, oder such as do bynde the freres most strongly togeder, bey the proffyte and commodytye comyng to the confrerie herfromme." Nothing can be plainer or more conclusive than the evidence which this affords of the existence of speculative Freemasonry, of the making and teaching of Masons, and of secrets peculiar to the craft. The concluding questions and answers—for the whole document is in the form of question and answer, as in an examination taken before the King—are as follows :—

"Are Maconnes gudder men then odhers?
"Some Maconnes are not so vertuous as some other menne, but

yn in the most parte, they be more gnde than they woulde be yf thay war not Maconnes.

"Doth Maconnes love eidher odher myghtylye, as beeth sayde ?

"Yea, verylyche, and yt may not odherwise be ; for gude menne and treu, kennynge eidher odher to be soche, doeth always love the more as they be more gude."

There is something in all this entirely different from what can be supposed concerning any ordinary operative guild. We have evidence here of Freemasonry, at least in its rudiments, however far it may have been from that comparative perfection to which it has now attained, and to which it may well be supposed that Ashmole, and after him Desaguliers and Anderson, in their respective times contributed. For it must be observed that Freemasonry is capable of indefinite improvement, and has continued to receive improvement even to the present day. Those who maintain its high antiquity are by no means bound to show that it was in every respect the same in former ages as it is now. All that they have to show is that it existed essentially the same, and that the Freemasons of the present day can trace their pedigree—if the figure may be allowed—to a remote antiquity. That they can go back beyond 1717, and even beyond the time of Ashmole in the middle of the seventeenth century, has now, it may be hoped, been sufficiently demonstrated.

"I know not what effect the sight of this old paper may have upon your Lordship," says Locke, in a note appended to his copy of it, which he sent to the Earl of Pembroke; "but for my own part I cannot deny that it has so much raised my curiosity, as to induce me to enter myself into the Fraternity, which I am determined to do (if I may be admitted) the next time I go to London, and that will be shortly." Whether or not the celebrated philosopher ever carried out this intention does not appear.

We have further evidence, however, of the existence and state of Freemasonry in the seventeenth century. The following regulations were adopted in 1663, the Earl of St Albans being Grand Master, Sir John Denham, Deputy

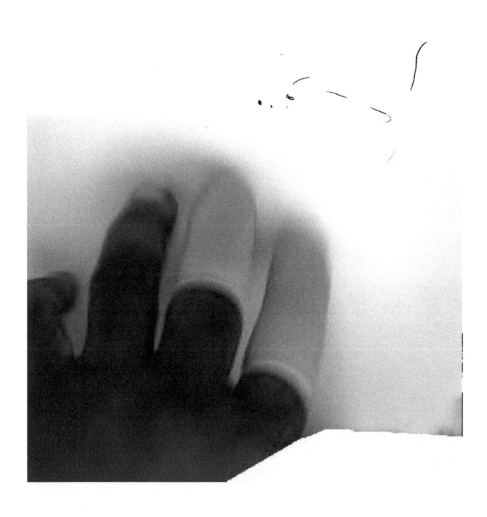

Grand Master, and Sir Christopher Wren and Mr George
Webb, Grand Wardens:—

" 1. That no person, of what degree soever, be accepted a Freemason, except in a regular Lodge, whereof one is to be a Master or
a Warden, in that division where such Lodge is kept, and another to
be a craftsman in Masonry.

" 2. That no person hereafter be accepted but such as are able of
body, of good parentage, of good reputation, and an observer of the
laws of the land.

" 3. That no person who shall be accepted a Freemason shall be
admitted into any Lodge until he has brought a certificate of the
time and place of his acceptation from the Master of the limit where
he was made and the Lodge kept; and the Master shall enroll the
same in parchment, and shall give an account of such acceptations
at every general assembly.

" 4. That every person who is now a Freemason shall bring to
the Master a note of the time of his acceptation, to the end that it
may be enrolled in such priority of place as the brother deserves,
and that the whole company and fellows may better know each
other.

" 5. That for the future, the said fraternity of Freemasons shall
be regulated and governed by one Grand Master and as many
Wardens as the said society shall think fit to appoint at every
general assembly.

" 6. That no person shall be accepted unless he be twenty-one
years old or upwards."

There can be no doubt but that we have in these regulations proof of a well-established system of Freemasonry in
1663. On the employment in them of the term *Freemason*,
it seems, for reasons already stated, of no particular
importance to insist. It may be asked, however, how the
view which they present of the state of Freemasonry in
England, immediately after the Restoration of Charles II.,
accords with that already exhibited of its low state at the
beginning of the eighteenth century? The answer is probably to be found in the troubles of the times, the political
convulsions which took away the attention of men from
those peaceful pursuits for which Masons are associated.

If, however, there seems to be a difficulty in reconciling our view of the state of Freemasonry in England in 1663 with that which existed forty or fifty years later, we find its truthfulness confirmed by the extracts from Ashmole's diary, already quoted, as well as by the letter of the London Lodges in 1717 to the other Lodges of England, and by the whole course of proceedings connected with the formation of the Grand Lodge of England in that year. The resolution then adopted by the Masons to choose a Grand Master among themselves, "till they should have the honour of a noble brother at their head," may of itself be held to imply the recollection of a time when that office was held by noble brethren. But how, it may be asked, can the Earl of St Albans have been Grand Master in 1663, when there was no regularly constituted Grand Lodge in England? Or how can Sir John Denham have been Deputy Grand Master, and Sir Christopher Wren and Mr George Webb, Grand Wardens? The probable answer is, that they were appointed by the King, or that the Grand Master was so appointed, and that he nominated the subordinate officers. For this seems to have been the practice in England, as well as in Scotland, till the end of the seventeenth century. It is stated, in masonic histories, that the Earl of St Albans was succeeded in the office of Grand Master by the Earl of Rivers, Sir Christopher Wren becoming Deputy Grand Master. If all this is not mere fable, the 1717 theory falls at once to the ground; and it becomes incumbent, therefore, on those who maintain that theory to prove that it is mere fable, and that these seemingly accurate historic statements have been fraudulently fabricated. Until proof of this is adduced, they must be accepted as true, and mere general declarations must be set aside as of no value whatever.

The following is the passage of Plot's " Natural History of Staffordshire," relative to Freemasonry. It is thought good to quote it in full, although it contains some things which might, perhaps, without impropriety have been omitted. But any abridgment of it might possibly be thought to diminish its value as evidence.   Having it before him at full length, and copied word for word, every reader may judge of its import for himself.

" They have a custom in Staffordshire, of admitting men into the Society of Freemasons, that in the morelands of this county seems to be of greater request than anywhere else, though I find the custom spread more or less all over the nation ; for here I found persons of the most eminent quality, that did not disdain to be of this fellowship; nor, indeed, need they, were it of that antiquity and honour that is pretended in a large parchment volume they have amongst them, containing the history and rules of the craft of Masonry, which is there deduced not only from sacred writ, but profane story ; particularly that it was brought into England by St Amphibalus, and first communicated to St Alban, who set down the charges of Masonry, and was made paymaster and governor of the king's works, and gave charges and manners as St Amphibalus had taught him : which were after confirmed by King Athelstan, whose youngest son, Edwyn, loved well Masonry, took upon him the charges, and learned the manners, and obtained for them of his father a free charter.   Whereupon he caused them to assemble at York, and to bring all the old books of their craft, and out of them ordained such charges and manners as they then thought fit, which charges in the said scroll, or parchment volume, are in part declared ; and thus was the craft of Masonry grounded and confirmed in England.   It is also there declared, that these charges and manners were after perused and approved by King Henry VI. and his council, both as to Masters and Fellows of this right worshipful craft.

" Into which society, when they are admitted, they call a meeting (or Lodge, as they term it in some places), which must consist at least of five or six of the ancients of the Order, whom the candidates present with gloves, and so likewise to their wives, and entertain with a collation, according to the custom of the place : this ended, they proceed to the admission of them, which chiefly consists in the communication of certain secret signs, whereby they are known to one another all over the nation, by which means they have maintenance whither ever they travel ; for if any man appear, though altogether unknown, that can show any of these signs to a Fellow of the society, whom they otherwise call an accepted Mason, he is obliged presently to come to him, from what company or place soever he be in ; nay, from the top of a steeple, what hazard or inconvenience soever he run, to know his pleasure, and assist him ; viz., if he want work, he is bound to find him some ; or if he cannot do that, to give him money, or otherwise support him till work can be had, which is one of their articles ; and it is another, that they advise the masters they work for, according to the best of their skill, acquainting them with the goodness or badness of their materials ; and if they be in any way out in the contrivance of the 'buildings, modestly to rectify them in it, that Masonry be not dishonoured ; and many such like that are commonly known ; but some others they have (to which they are sworn, after their fashion) that none know but themselves, which I have reason to suspect are much worse than these, perhaps as bad as this history of the craft itself ; than which there is nothing I ever met more false or incoherent.

"For not to mention that St Amphibalus, by judicious persons, is thought rather to be the cloak than master of St Alban ; or how unlikely it is that St Alban himself, in such a barbarous age, and in times of persecution, should be supervisor of any works. It is plain that King Athelstan was never married, or ever had so much as any natural issue (unless we give way to the fabulous history of Guy, Earl of Warwick, whose eldest son, Reynburn, is said, indeed, to have been married to Leoneat, the supposed daughter of Athelstan, which will not serve the turn neither), much less ever had he a lawful son Edwyn, of whom I find not the least umbrage in history. He had, indeed, a brother of that name, of whom he was so jealous, though very young when he came to the crown, that he sent him to sea in a pinnace, without tackle or oar, only in company with a page, that his death might be imputed to the waves, and not to him ; whence the young prince, not able to master his passions, cast himself headlong into the sea, and there died. Who how unlikely to learn their manners, to get them a charter, or to call them together at York, let the reader judge.

"Yet more improbable it is still, that Henry VI. and his council, should ever peruse or approve their charges and manners, and so confirm these right worshipful Masters and Fellows, as they are called in the scroll ; for in the third year of his reign, when he could not be four years old, I find an Act of Parliament abolishing this society ; it being then ordained, that no congregations and confederacies should be made by Masons, in their general chapters and assemblies whereby the good course and effect of the statutes of labourers were violated and broken in subversion of law ; and that those who caused such chapters or congregations to be holden, should be adjudged felons; and those Masons that came to them should be punished by imprisonment, and make fine and ransom, at the King's will. So very much out was the compiler of this history of the craft of Masonry, and so little skill had he in our chronicles and laws. Which statute, though repealed by a subsequent act in the fifth of Elizabeth, where servants and labourers are compelled to serve, and their wages limited ; and all masters made punished for giving more wages than is taxed by the justices, and the servants if they take it, &c.; yet this act too being but little observed, it is still to be feared these chapters of Freemasons do as much mischief as before, which, if one may estimate by the penalty, was anciently so great, that perhaps it might be useful to examine them now."— " *Natural History of Staffordshire*," pp. 316–318.

Plot's account of Freemasonry, as it existed in his day, is all the more worthy of being accepted as evidence bearing on the question now specially under consideration, and on the whole question of the antiquity of Freemasonry, that he was evidently under the influence of strong prejudice against the whole system. This seems extraordinary in one whose patron was Elias Ashmole ; but the passage just quoted exhibits the fact too strongly for any possibility of doubt. His antipathy was evidently very strong, and when he could allege nothing bad against Freemasonry, he took leave to say that he suspected it. He felt himself constrained to state some of the laws of Freemasonry which no man can deny to be but excellent and honourable, but he had " reason to suspect" that some of its secrets were very bad. What reason, he says not. It would be waste of time and of paper to debate on such a question against such an antagonist ; nor is greater respect due to his arguments concerning the early history of Freemasonry in England. It is not necessary for us—in so far as our present purpose is concerned—to show into what errors he has fallen as to the relation of Henry VI. to Freemasonry, or as to the history of Athelstan, and Edwyn, and St Alban. Much here may be legendary and fabulous, whilst there is a substratum of truth. But we need not inquire.

In so far as the 1717 theory is concerned, which alone is at present under discussion, it is enough for us to have proof from Plot's pages, that Freemasonry existed in England in the reign of James II., in the year 1686, when his book was published, and before it, having a system substantially the same with that of the present day. A more perfect demolition of the 1717 theory than it affords, could not be possibly desired. We find from Plot's account of the Freemasonry of his day—at least thirty-one years before 1717—that Lodges of Masons existed not only in Staffordshire, but throughout England; that they were governed by laws such as those of our present Freemasonry, maintaining the same system of brotherly kindness, and the same system of secrecy in the tokens by which the members of the Order could make themselves known to each other; that persons of " the most eminent quality " sought admission into the Order, and that they claimed for their Order a great antiquity. We find that the same controversy then existed as to the antiquity of the Order which is carried on at the present day—only, of course, it had no reference to 1717, nor to Desaguliers and Anderson, who, if they were then born, had not yet appeared in any public capacity. It is very interesting to see an antagonist of Freemasonry in 1686 raising objections against the antiquity of the system much like those urged in 1871; although in 1871 we are confidently told that it does not extend back to 1686 at all. We take Plot's evidence that it does; none more conclusive could be desired.

A curious corroborative proof of the antiquity of Freemasonry, not only in Britain, but on the Continent of Europe, is to be found in Plot's statement regarding the gloves presented by the candidates to the "ancients of the Order" who constitute the Lodge that admits them. This practice has been long discontinued in Britain; and although a law is still in force for the "clothing" by the brethren of the Lodge, it is observed in a different manner. But the presentation of gloves is still the practice in some parts of Europe. From this we may infer that it is an ancient practice, derived from a time when there existed a close connection between the Freemasonry of England and of the Continent. It would not be easy to account for this minute point of agreement between the practice of England in 1686, and of some parts of the Continent at the present day, without supposing an ancient connection and a common origin.

What the "scroll" or "parchment" was, of which Plot speaks, it would not be easy, and it is not necessary, to determine. Some have supposed that it is the same MS. to which Locke's letter refers, and which in his time existed in the Bodleian Library at Oxford. This opinion is not supported by sufficient evidence; but the reference made to Henry VI. and his connection with Freemasonry give it considerable probability. If not the same, it must have been of somewhat similar purport.

The Harleian MS., No. 2054, in the British Museum, belongs to the early part of the seventeenth century. It is in the handwriting of Randle Holmes. It was found at Chester. It contains the names of the brethren received into the Masonic fraternity, with what sum of money each was required to pay, or, as the phrase in the MS. is, to "give for to be a Freemason." Here, again, we find the use of the term Freemason at a more early date than it is convenient for some who have recently founded their arguments upon it to assign to it. This MS. affords also some evidence of the existence of a system of Freemasonry at the time when it was written, similar to that of the present day. It informs us that there are "several words and signes of a Freemason to be reveiled, . . . which may be communicated to no one except to the Master and Fellows of the said society of Freemasons." Brethren initiated will at once understand this. There were never any such words or signs among the tailors, or the shoemakers, or any of the other crafts.

Many of the Lodges throughout England have records long previous to 1717; which, whilst they prove the antiquity of the Lodge, show also its continuity, and, that in the estimation of all the members, they continued after the foundation of the Grand Lodge of England, and their connection with it, to be the same Lodges as before, and to carry out the same system as before. The Master's chair of one of the English Lodges was probably made in the early part of the seventeenth century, if it is not even older, and it bears symbols similar to those now used in Masonic Lodges. These are important facts, as bearing on the question now at issue.

Reference has already been made to the large number of noblemen and other persons of eminence who joined the Masonic fraternity in England very soon after the revival of Freemasonry, and the foundation of the present Grand Lodge in 1717. It may be proper, however, to direct a little further attention to this point. It has been mentioned that the Masons having resolved to choose one of their own existing number for Grand Master, " till they should have the honour of a noble brother at their head," their choice fell upon Brother Anthony Sayer. He was succeeded by George Payne, Esq., and he by Dr John Theophilus Desaguliers; the office being held by each only for one year. Desaguliers was succeeded by Mr Payne, who was re-elected Grand Master, and contributed more than perhaps any other to the advancement of the interests of the fraternity. But in 1721 the Duke of Montague was elected Grand Master, and from that time to the present the office has always been filled by persons of high rank, sometimes by members of the Royal Family, and even by the King himself. The Duke of Montague was succeeded in 1722 by the Duke of Wharton, and he in 1723 by the Earl of Dalkeith, afterwards Duke of Buccleuch. But it is unnecessary to proceed in this enumeration of names. These are only mentioned as showing to how high a position Freemasonry in England attained within two or three years after 1717, and how unreasonable, therefore, the supposition is that it was then newly invented, and that its pretensions of antiquity were wholly unfounded, or that it was a thing which had never been heard of before. The only theory which consists with the facts is, that it had a prior existence, and that its pretensions to high antiquity were not new, nor then brought forward for the first time.

THE rapid extension of Freemasonry in Britain and other countries, after the foundation of the Grand Lodge of England in 1717, confirms the argument derived from the speedy accession of noblemen and other persons of distinction to the masonic body. It cannot reasonably be imagined that a newly-invented scheme, however ingenious, should have at once received the approbation of men in all parts of Britain ; but we find Lodges already existing in all parts of the country at once to have cordially accepted it, and new Lodges to have been formed on the same principles. The only supposition which can be entertained is, that the old Lodges recognised in it the system on which they had originally been founded, and that therefore Masons in all parts of the kingdom gladly acknowledged the new Grand Lodge, and attached themselves to it. The extension of Masonry after 1717 was very rapid in England; in 1730 the Grand Lodge of Ireland was founded, and the Grand Lodge of Scotland in 1736. The foundation of the Grand Lodge of Scotland took place under circumstances already partially referred to, and which sufficiently indicate the connection of the modern Freemasonry carried on by the Grand Lodge and the affiliated Lodges in Scotland with a more ancient Freemasonry existing in that country. William St Clair, of Roslin, finding it necessary to part with his estate of Roslin, with the possession of which his tenure of the office of Grand Master was connected, according to the original grant from James II. of Scotland, and having at heart the interests of the Order of Freemasons, resolved to resign his office, at the same time recommending that the Masons of Scotland should form a Grand Lodge and elect for themselves a Grand Master. The following letter was, therefore, sent by the Lodges in Edinburgh and its neighbourhood to all the Lodges in Scotland, inviting them to appear on next St Andrew's Day, by themselves or their

representatives, to take part in the election of a Grand
Master :—

"BRETHREN,—The four Lodges in and about Edinburgh, having
taken into their serious consideration the great loss that Masonry
has sustained through the want of a Grand Master, authorised us
to signify to you, our good and worthy brethren, our hearty desire
and firm intention to choose a Grand Master for Scotland ; and in
order that the same may be done with the greatest harmony, we
hereby invite you (as we have done all the regular Lodges known by
us) to concur in such a great and good work, whereby, it is to be
hoped, Masonry may be restored to its ancient lustre in this kingdom ; and, for effectuating this laudable design, we humbly desire
that, betwixt this and Martinmas-day next, you will be pleased to
give us a brotherly answer in relation to the election of a Grand
Master, which we propose to be on St Andrew's Day for the first
time, and ever thereafter to be on St John the Baptist's Day, or as
the Grand Lodge shall appoint by the majority of voices, which are
to be collected from the Masters and Wardens of all the regular
Lodges then present, or by proxy to any Master Mason or fellow craft
in any Lodge in Scotland, and the election is to be in Mary's Chapel.
All that is hereby proposed is for the advancement and prosperity
of Masonry, in its greatest and most charitable perfection. We
hope and expect a suitable return ; wherein, if any Lodges are
defective, they have themselves only to blame. We heartily wish
you all manner of success and prosperity, and ever are, with great
respect, your affectionate and loving brethren," &c.

Now, let it be remembered that this letter was written
scarcely nineteen years after the foundation of the Grand
Lodge of England, and let us see how it bears on the 1717
theory, the theory which ascribes the origin of modern Freemasonry to the date of the foundation of that Grand Lodge.
We must bear in mind that there was then no such intimate
connection between England and Scotland as, through rail-
ways and telegraphs, exists at the present day, and therefore
the foundation of the Grand Lodge in England was not likely
to have such immediate effect in the northern part of the
island as might now be expected from such an event. Let
us look at the letter of the Lodges of Edinburgh and its

neighbourhood, keeping these circumstances in view. We see in it evidence of the existence of a system of Freemasonry long anterior to its date. It is plainly written on the assumption that such a system has long existed, and is known as already in existence by those to whom it is addressed. And these are not individuals scattered throughout Scotland, but regularly organised Lodges, the existence of which is proof sufficient of the prior existence of a system of Masonry in Scotland. We have this proof, in fact, in the existence of the Lodges in Edinburgh and its neighbourhood, which united to send the letter, and in that of the Lodges to which it is addressed. Can any reasonable man suppose that all this had sprung up after 1717, and in consequence of the action of Dr Desaguliers and Dr Anderson? The letter of the Edinburgh Masons in 1736 plainly proceeds on the assumption of an ancient system recognised as existing, and in the advancement of which the brethren throughout the country are expected to take an interest. We find also that thirty-two Lodges responded to the call, and concurred in the formation of the Grand Lodge of Scotland. The very names of some of these Lodges are indicative of antiquity, and of connection with a system not of very recent introduction, as that of the Canongate Kilwinning,—the Kilwinning Scotch Arms,—the Kilwinning, Leith,—the Kilwinning, Glasgow,—Kilwinning, Torphichen, &c. It is easy for the advocates of the 1717 theory to ridicule the pretensions of the Kilwinning Lodge—Mother Kilwinning—to high antiquity, as its oldest records have unhappily been destroyed or lost; but it is not so easy to get over the fact of the existence of Lodges which profess to have derived their charters from it, and which have assumed its name, as a name of honourable distinction, in their own. That Lodges so designated existed in 1736, is clear enough from the records connected with the foundation of the Grand Lodge of Scotland, and this is enough for our present purpose. That these Lodges were founded after 1717, and owed their origin to the movement which took place in England in that year, is a notion too ridiculous to require serious consideration.   And if they are acknowledged, as they must be, to have had a prior existence, or to have derived their origin from some other source, the argument against the 1717 theory is conclusive.

The further proceedings of the Masons of Scotland in 1736 consist with the theory of the antiquity of Freemasonry, and are utterly inconsistent with that of its novel origin.   They received from William St Clair of Roslin a renunciation of his rights as their patron, protector, judge, or Master; and, in the deed of resignation, he assigns as a reason for it that his "holding or claiming any such jurisdiction, right, or privilege, might be prejudicial to the craft and vocation of Masonry"—"of which," he says, "I am a member."   If Masonry was a mere novelty in Scotland in 1736, William St Clair of Roslin must have laboured under a strange mistake, and the other Masons of Scotland must have been mistaken along with him.   All this, however, and much more of the same nature, is implied in the maintenance of the 1717 theory.   William St Clair of Roslin must have made his deed of renunciation of his ancient hereditary rights under a delusion, and the Masons of Scotland must have accepted it under a delusion, believing their order and their Lodges to have had an ancient existence, whilst in fact they had newly sprung into being!

We have, however, another proof of the existence of Freemasonry in Scotland long before the beginning of the seventeenth century in the Lodge St John, Melrose, the oldest existing records of which are prior to the year 1600. The older records of the Lodge have been lost, but those existing suffice for the purpose of our present argument. The St John Lodge, Melrose, has never connected itself with the Grand Lodge of Scotland, but has maintained an independent existence, claiming an antiquity even greater than that of the Kilwinning Lodge, known in Scottish Freemasonry as "Mother Kilwinning," from which other Lodges are proud to have derived their charters, and to deduce their connection.   Its working, however, has been entirely in accordance with that of the Grand Lodge, and the Lodges holding of it. In this respect it perfectly corresponds in its system of Freemasonry with the system ordinarily prevalent in Scotland. That it has records dating from the latter part of the sixteenth century is enough for our purpose, as establishing the fact of the existence of Freemasonry in Scotland at that date, and exploding the 1717 theory. The records of the Masonic Lodge at Melrose also plainly show that amongst its members and its Masters were persons of high consideration in the district—not operative masons, as the exigencies of the 1717 theory would require.

THE extension of Freemasonry throughout the world was very rapid after the foundation of the Grand Lodge of England. Lodges were founded in the British colonies, in India, and in many countries of Europe. It is not necessary here to state in detail the circumstances which attended the foundation of these Lodges. That the impulse was given from England is not to be denied, and every brother must gratefully acknowledge the obligations of the order to Desaguliers, Anderson, Payne, and others, who contributed so much to the revival of the system, the excellence of which they appreciated. Nothing, however, can be more incredible than the notion that a perfectly new system, essentially different from anything that had formerly existed, was thus rapidly and widely extended. The contrary supposition commends itself at once to the mind, that there existed throughout the world a system of Masonry, of which that propagated from England was acknowledged as an improvement, but upon the foundation of which it was established. On any other theory it is impossible to account for the formation of Mason Lodges in different parts of the continent of Europe in the early part of the eighteenth century, and for the constancy of their members under persecution, to which in several countries they were subjected.

It has been alleged that Freemasonry was introduced into France by British refugees after the Revolution of 1688. There is no reason to doubt that the Jacobites who fled from Britain at that time carried with them their Freemasonry, but there is good reason to believe that they found it already existing in France. In 1645, forty-three years before the Revolution in England, a particular jurisdiction of Masonry—*Maçonnerie*—was established in France. It related especially to the questions concerning operative Masonry, which, however, was thus distinguished from every other operative industry, and the Masons were entitled to appeal to the Parliament of Paris, in which their advocates were allowed to plead. The high and peculiar distinction thus granted to them is worthy of consideration. It shows that a system of Masonry existed in France in the middle of the seventeenth century, upon which the improvements introduced from England at a later date might be grafted. At what date they were introduced, it is impossible to say, but there is reason to think that it was before 1717. About the beginning of the eighteenth century the French gave a singular pre-eminence to Scottish Masonry, and added the title of *Chevalier Maçon Ecossais* to the three symbolical degrees of Masonry. The French Masons invented new degrees and made other innovations in the system of Freemasonry not consistent with its principles and original design. Their Lodges also were transmuted into political clubs, a fact not difficult to be accounted for when the political circumstances of the time are considered, but inconsistent with all the principles of Freemasonry, and, in the end, most hurtful, because it led to the entertainment in high quarters of most erroneous opinions as to the nature and tendencies of Freemasonry. The assemblies of Freemasons were prohibited by royal edict in France in 1737, on the pretence that beneath their inviolable secrets they might cover some design hostile to religion and dangerous to the kingdom. The edict, however, was not enforced, and Masonry continued to flourish in France throughout the latter part of the eighteenth century.

It is not necessary here to give a particular account of the spread of Freemasonry in the British colonies and on the continent of Europe. A few sentences from Laurie's " History of Freemasonry " may suffice, as bearing upon the present argument, and showing the extreme improbability of the notion that the whole system was originated in 1717:—

"In 1729," Laurie says, " it was introduced into the East Indies, and a short time after a Provincial Grand Master was appointed to superintend the Lodges in that quarter. In 1730 the Grand Lodge of Ireland was instituted ; Lodges were erected in different parts of America ; and a provincial deputation granted to Monsieur Thuanus for the circle of Lower Saxony. In 1731 a patent was sent from England to erect a Lodge at the Hague, in which Francis Stephen, Duke of Lorraine, afterwards Emperor of Germany, was initiated, and Provincial Grand Masters were appointed for Russia and Andalusia in Spain. In 1736 Lodges were erected at Geneva and Cape Coast in Africa, and provincial deputations were granted for Upper Saxony and the American islands. In 1738 a Lodge was instituted at Brunswick under the patronage of the Grand Lodge of Scotland, in which Frederick III. of Prussia was initiated when Prince Royal ; and so pleased was his Highness with the maxims and ceremonies of the order, that he ever afterwards was its most zealous supporter, and even requested that a Lodge should be erected in the capital of his dominions. . In this Lodge many of the German Princes were initiated, who afterwards filled the office of Grand Master with much honour to themselves and advantage to the fraternity."—*Laurie's " History of Freemasonry,"* edition of 1859, p. 61.

It is difficult to imagine that all this resulted from the inventive genius of Dr Desaguliers and Dr Anderson. The more probable theory is that there existed in Germany, Russia, and Spain, as well as in France, and so in fact throughout Europe, a system of Masonry, of which their revival and improvement were readily accepted. How otherwise the system could have been accepted at all, and that so widely and generally, it is impossible to conceive. Those who maintain the 1717 theory are certainly bound to adduce the most positive evidence in support of it, and this they have hitherto failed to do.

The persecutions of Freemasonry in different parts of Europe afford us another argument of the same kind. Would men, it may be asked, have endured persecution, and still continued faithful to their masonic obligations, if these had had no other origin than the inventive genius of Dr Desaguliers or of Elias Ashmole? Would they have felt them of any such force as facts show that

they did?   Would not the whole thing have seemed
to them ridiculous?   And although at first it might
have attracted them as a novelty, would they not have
flung it away when it came to be placed in competition
with liberty and fortune, as was sometimes the case?
It is no reply to this argument to say that they were
deceived?   For, in the first place, there is no proof of
any intention to deceive ; in the second place, there is no
imaginable motive for deception ; and in the third place, a
deception so successful and extensive cannot reasonably
be supposed possible.   If men had not been convinced of
the truth and value of the system, they would have given
up the contest at once.   They did not do so; they
maintained it as a good and useful system,—and surely many
of them must have been men of intelligence, as capable
of judging as their successors at the present day.

"These persecutions," Laurie says, "took their rise in Holland in
the year 1735.   The States-General were alarmed at the rapid
increase of Freemasons, who held their meetings in every town
under their government ; and as they could not believe that architecture and brotherly love were their only objects, they resolved to
discountenance their proceedings.   In consequence of this determina-
tion, an edict was issued by Government, stating that though they
had discovered nothing in the practices of the fraternity either
injurious to the interests of the Republic, or contrary to the
character of good citizens, yet, in order to prevent any bad conse-
quences which might ensue from such associations, they deemed it
prudent to abolish their assemblies.   Notwithstanding this prohibi-
tion, a respectable Lodge having continued to meet at Amsterdam,
intelligence was communicated to the authorities, who arrested all
the members, and brought them to the tribunal of justice.   Before
this tribunal, in presence of all the magistrates of the city, the
Masters and Wardens boldly defended themselves, and declared upon
oath that they were loyal subjects, faithful to their religion, and
zealous for the interests of their country ; that Freemasonry was an
institution venerable in itself, and useful to society ; and that, though
they could not reveal the secrets and ceremonies, they would assure
them that they were contrary neither to the laws of God nor man ;
that they would willingly admit into their order any one of their

number, from whom they would receive such information as would
satisfy any reasonable mind.   In consequence of these declarations
the brethren were dismissed, and the town-secretary requested to
become a member of the fraternity.   After initiation, he returned
to the court of justice, and gave such a favourable account of the
principles and practice of the Society that all the magistrates became
brethren and patrons of the fraternity."—*Laurie,* pp. 61, 62.

Had this story related to a remote period, as the
twelfth or thirteenth century, it would doubtless have been
ridiculed as incredible; but as it relates to last century,
this is out of the question.   However, it is important
to observe that its date is only eighteen years after that
memorable one, 1717 ; and every one can judge for himself
if it is likely that a newly invented system, introduced by
imposture in London in 1717, would have acquired such
strength in 1735 at Amsterdam.

The persecutions of the Freemasons in different parts of
Europe in the latter part of the eighteenth century show
how strongly the system had taken root, and how determined its adherents were to maintain it.   In 1738, a Papal
bull was issued against all Freemasons, and all who
promoted or favoured their cause.   This bull was followed
by an edict, dated 17th January 1739, condemning all Freemasons in the Papal States to the galleys, the rack, and a
fine of a thousand crowns in gold.   In consequence of these
enactments at Rome, the Roman Catholic clergy of Holland, in 1740, attempted to enforce obedience to the commands of their superiors.   " It was customary among the
priests of that country to examine the religious qualifications of those who requested a certificate to receive the Holy
Sacrament.   Taking advantage of their spiritual power,
they concluded the examination of the candidates by asking
if they were Freemasons.   If they were, the certificate was
refused, and they were expelled for ever from the communion-table."—*Laurie's " History of Freemasonry,"* p. 64.
But the States-General interfered, finding that respectable
men were thus shut out from the communion-table, and

prohibited the priests from asking questions that were not connected with the religious character of the applicants.

It would be easy to go on, showing the persecutions to which Freemasons were subjected in different parts of Europe during the latter half of the eighteenth century. It is, however, unnecessary. A mere example or two will serve the present purpose as well as a full and detailed account. That purpose is to show that Freemasonry must have existed for a long time prior to 1717, and that it did not spring into existence on the Continent of Europe by mere transplantation from England, but found its origin in an ancient system long prevalent there. Not otherwise can we reasonably account for the extension of the order, for its being joined by princes and nobles, for the endurance of persecution by its members. All these things being considered, it seems utterly incredible that Dr Desaguliers and Dr Anderson invented and introduced a new system, but, on the contrary, in the highest degree probable, that they found, as they said, a system already existing, which they deemed it worthy of their utmost exertions to extend.

We must now go farther back in the history of Masonry, and inquire into its existence and nature in centuries previous to the sixteenth. We shall find important aid in the ancient charges preserved in a MS. in possession of the Lodge of Antiquity in London, and written in the reign of James II. of England. The date of the MS. thus appears to belong to the latter part of the seventeenth century, although the charges must be supposed to be really of much more ancient date,—how much more ancient it is not necessary for the present purpose to inquire. In fact, in so far as the 1717 theory is concerned, it is enough to show that these charges existed in the latter part of the seventeenth century, and that they manifest the existence of a system of Masonry essentially the same with that which now exists, not a system pertaining to a mere operative craft or guild. The proof of this is best to be found in the charges themselves, and therefore they are here subjoined :—

" Every man that is a Mason take good heed to these charges (wee pray), that if any man find himself guilty of any of these charges, he may amend himselfe, or principally for dread of God. You that be charged, take good heed that you keep these charges well ; for it is a great evill for a man to forswear himself upon a book.

" The first charge is, That yee shall be true men to God and the Holy Church, and to use no error or heresie by your understanding, and by wise men's teaching.

" Allso, secondly, That yee shall be true liegemen to the King of England, without treason or any falsehood, and that yee know no .reason or treachery, but yee shall give notice thereof to the King, or to his counsell ; also yee shall be true one to another—that is to say, every Mason to the craft that is Mason allowed ; yee shall doe to him as yee would be done unto yourselfe.

" Thirdly, And ye shall keepe truly all the counsell that ought to be kept in the way of Masonhood, and all the counsell of the Lodge or of the Chamber. Allso, that ye shall be no thief, nor thieves, to your knowledge free; that yee shall be true to the king, lord, or master that yee serve, and truely to see and worke to his advantage.

" Fourthly, Yee shall call Masons your fellows, or your brethren, and no other names.

" Fifthly, Yee shall not take your fellow's wife in villany, nor deflower his daughter or servant, nor put him to no disworship.

" Sixthly, Yee shall truely pay for your meat or drinke, wheresoever ye goe, to table or board. Allso, ye shall do no villany whereby the craft, or science may be slandered.

" These be the charges general to every true Mason, both Masters and Fellows."

It is evident enough from these charges that the system of Masonry in the seventeenth century had in it peculiarities which distinguished it from mere operative crafts. No such care was exercised by any other craft or guild as to the morals of their members; but here we find morality put in the first place, if indeed religion may not be said to precede it— religion and morality, however, are inseparable, and morality is properly based upon religion. The Mason is required to be a true man to God and the Holy Church, and to use no error or heresy by his understanding and by wise men's teaching. In what other craft, it may be asked,—in what other guild were such charges ever framed? Until this question is answered, by the production of sufficient evidence, we must hold that Masonry had a peculiar position in the seventeenth century, very different from that of ordinary crafts and guilds, and that, in fact, it was of a nature very different.

We may, however, go on to quote the remainder of the charges, of which the first part has just been given; and whilst we see in them evidence of the relation of the whole system to operative Masonry, we shall see further evidence that it was something more :—

" Now I will rehearse other charges single for Masons allowed or accepted.

" First, That no Mason take on him no lord's worke, nor other man's, so that the craft have no slander.

" Secondly, Allso, that no master take worke but that he take reasonable pay for itt ; so that the lord may be truely served, and the master to live honestly, and to pay his fellows truely.   And that no master or fellow supplant others of their worke—that is to say, that if he have taken a worke, or else stand master of any worke, that he shall not put him out, unless he unable of cunning to make an ende of his worke.   And no Master nor Fellow shall take an apprentice for less than seven years.   And that the apprentice be free-born, and of limbs whole as a man ought to be, and no bastard.   And that no Master or Fellow take no allowance to be made Mason without the assent of his fellows, at least six or seven.

" Thirdly, That he that be made be able in all degrees—that is, free-born, of good kindred, true, and no bondsman, and that he have his right limbs as a man ought to have.

" Fourthly, That no Master take an apprentice unless he have occupation to occupy two or three fellows at the least.

" Fifthly, That no Master or Fellow put away any lord's worke to taske that ought to be journey-worke.

" Sixthly, That every master give pay to his fellows and servants as they may deserve, soe that he be not defamed with false working. And that none slander another behind his backe, to make him lose his good name.

" Seventhly, That no Fellow in the house or abroad answer another ungodly or reproveably without a cause.

" Eighthly, That every Master Mason doe reverence to his elder ; and that a Mason be no common plaier at the cards, dice, or hazard, nor at any other unlawful plaies, through the which the science and craft may be dishonoured and slandered.

" Ninthly, That no Fellow goe into the town by night, except he have a Fellow with him, who may bear him record that he was in an honest place.

" Tenthly, That every Master and Fellow shall come to the assemblie, if itt be within three miles of him, if he have any warning. And if he have trespassed against the craft, to abide the award of the Master and Fellows.

" Eleventhly, That every Master and Fellow that hath trespassed against the craft shall stand to the correction of other Masters and Fellows, to make him accord ; and if they cannot accord, to go to the common law.

" Twelfthly, That a Master or Fellow make not a mould-stone, square, nor rule, to no lowen, nor let no lowen worke within their lodge, nor without, to mould-stone.

" Thirteenthly, That every Mason receive and cherish strange fellows when they come over.the countrie, and set them on worke if they will worke, as the manner is—that is to say, if the Mason have any mould-stone in his place, he shall give him a mould-stone, and sett him on worke ; and if he have none, the Mason shall refresh him with money unto the next Lodge.

" Fourteenthly, That every Mason shall truely serve his master for his pay.

" Fifteenthly, That every Master shall truely make an end of his worke. taske, or journey, wheresoe it be.

" These be all the charges and covenants that ought to be read at the installment of Master, or making of a Freemason or Freemasons. The Almighty God of Jacob, who ever have you and me in His keeping, bless us now and ever. Amen."

Now it may be granted at once that all this relates to operative Masonry ; but it cannot be granted that it relates to operative Masonry alone, or to a mere operative craft, such as that of tailors or shoemakers. There is no evidence of any such rules laid down for any such craft. Here, however, we find Masons laid under obligations of the highest morality, not only in their relations to one another, but to all around them, and bound above all to be true men to God and the Holy Church, to " use no error or heresy," and to be true liegemen to the King. It is unnecessary to point out how in further respects the moral law is enforced; but the question may again be asked of those who regard Masonry as having been a mere common craft in the seventeenth century, what other craft had any such rules? or in what craft any such regard was paid to the character and conduct of members? It has been a peculiar distinction of the masonic fraternity, from the most ancient times to which its origin can be traced, that it has insisted on the strictest scrutiny into the character and conduct of those asking admission into it; and that it has exercised supervision over its members as to their observance of the moral law, and their obedience to the law of the land.

The charges which have just been quoted are very similar to those contained in the celebrated *York Constitutions*. We need not enter into the disputed question of the authenticity of these York Constitutions. It matters not to our present inquiry whether they are of the date A.D. 926, or much more recent. It is enough that they are of a date anterior to the beginning of the eighteenth century, and this cannot be disputed. The whole question will be found discussed in Findel's "History of Freemasonry," in which, certainly, no inclination is shown to maintain the antiquity of documents, or of anything connected with the masonic system; and the conclusion appears to be, that although the date A.D. 926 may be imaginary, yet the York Constitutions must be referred to a date of considerable antiquity. That they are older than the beginning of the eighteenth century must be admitted; unless it is supposed that they were fabricated by Desaguliers, Anderson, and their fellows, in order to carry out their scheme of Freemasonry, a supposition not for a moment to be entertained, when the characters of the men are considered, or when it is considered that the scheme presented to them no advantage whatever, that they had nothing to gain by its success.

It may be well to give here the words of the York Constitutions, although they are so similar to those already quoted :—

"(1.) The first charge is, That yee shall be true men to God and to the Holy Church, and to use no error or heresie by your understanding and by wise men's teaching.

"(2.) That yee shall be true liegemen to the King, without treason or any falsehood, and that yee know no treason or treachery, but ye shall give knowledge thereof to the King, or to his counsel.

"(3.) Yee shall be obliging towards all men, and as far as yee can establish true friendship with them, nor mind when they are attached to another religion or set of opinions.

"(4.) Allso yee shall be true each one to other—that is to say, to every Mason of the science of Masonry that bene Masons allowed; yee shall doe to them as yee would that they should doe to you.

Should any brother have trespassed against the craft, or against one of the brethren, all his fellow-masons must stand by him, to make compensation for his trespass, that he may grow better.

"(5.) Yee shall keepe truly all the counsells of Lodge and Chamber, and all other counsells that ought to be kept by way of Masonhood, and to keepe the signe from every man that is not a brother.

"(6.) And also that noe Mason shall be in thefte or thievishe, for as far forthe as he may weete or know; that ye shall be true to the lord or master that yee serve, and truely to see and worke for his advantage.

"(7.) Yee shall truly pay for your meat or drinke, whersoever ye go, to table or bord. Also, yee shall do no villany there, whereby the craft or science may be slandered.

"(8.) That no Mason take on him no lord's worke, nor any other man's, unlesse he knowe himselfe well able to performe the worke, so that the craft have no slander; also, that noe Master Mason take noe worke, but that he take it reasonable, soe that the lorde may be truly served with his own goode, and the Master to live honestly, and to paie his fellows truly their paie as the manner is.

"(9.) That no Master or fellow supplant others of their worke, that is to say, that if he hath taken a worke, or else stand Master of any worke, that he shall not put him out, unless he unable of cunning to make an end of his worke.

"(10.) And no Master nor fellow shall take no apprentice for less than seven years. And that no Master or fellow take no allowance to be made Mason without the assent of his fellows, at least six or seven.

"(11.) And that the apprentice be free-born, and of limbs whole as a man ought to be.

"(12.) Also that no fellow blame another, if he knowe not himself better how to doe it, than he whom he blameth.

"(13.) And also that no fellowe, within the Lodge or without, misanswer any other ungodly or reprovably without reasonable cause; and that every Mason shall reverence his elder, and put him to worshippe.

"(14.) Also that every Mason be obedient to the rulers and patrons of the order of Masonry, and performe willingly what they are bid.

"(15.) That every Mason receive and cherish strange fellowes when they come over the countries, and give the signe, and set them on worke, if they will worke, as the manner is. He shall help his

needy brother, when he knoweth of his need, as the manner, an it
be within half a mile of him.

"(16.) Also that no Master or fellow shall receive in the Lodge
any other that is not made a Mason, that he lerne to make no molde
or squyar nor rule to noe layer, nor set noe layer within the Lodge,
ne without, to hew or molde stones.

"These are the charges which ye shall keepe, so help you God,
and your holydome, and by this booke unto your power.   What in
the future shall be found good and useful, shall be written down,
and, by the rulers and patrons be made known that all the brethren
may truly hold and keepe them."

Once more, and for the last time, let us try to imagine a
guild of tailors or shoemakers having rules such as these.
The term *craft* might be employed, but the term *science*
would not likely be.   We find both employed in these York
Constitutions; and whatever may be their date, they plainly
show that Masonry, whilst it was an operative craft, was
something more than a mere operative craft at the time
when they were drawn up.

OF great importance in the argument concerning the antiquity of Freemasonry, and particularly concerning the existence of the Masonic system and Order before 1717, and of the continued existence of that system and Order after that date, without essential change, is the fact of the regard generally paid by Freemasons to the Festivals of St John the Baptist and St John the Evangelist. How is this to be accounted for, but on the ground that an old system was maintained and perpetuated, retaining its old characteristic features, and all that its reformers—if so they may be called—deemed its innocent peculiarities. The Masons of England and other countries, during the days of the prevalence of the Roman Catholic religion, had always recognised St John the Baptist and St John the Evangelist as their patron saints, paying special regard to their festivals, and in most places, if not in all, holding their chief meetings upon them. This practice was continued in England, Scotland, and other countries, even after the Reformation, Freemasonry being slow to make any changes but such as were absolutely necessary. We find, therefore, after the year 1717, and the revival of Freemasonry in England, these festivals still observed with special regard, the meetings of the Lodges held in connection with them, and the names of these saints adopted in the names of Lodges, not only in the more ancient, but also in the more recent Lodges. It could not be easy to account for this on any other theory than that of continued connection, of the continued existence of the older Lodges, and the perpetuation of an ancient system of Freemasonry. It is impossible to imagine that Dr Desaguliers, Dr Anderson, and their coadjutors, being zealous Protestants, as we know they were, should have introduced into a system devised by them a set of saints' days and saints' names, appointing the festivals of these saints to be specially observed. But it is easy to suppose—for it is the natural supposition—that finding these already incorporated in the system which they thought so excellent as to be worthy of general recommendation, they permitted them to remain, and so to be carried wherever the Order extended, as all the world knows that they have been.

As proof how extensive was the regard for the festival of St John the Baptist among Masons, I may be permitted to quote the following extract from the records of the Brechin Lodge (Brechin St Ninian's), Scotland, of date 27th December 1714 :—

" It is statute and ordained that every member of the Lodge duly and strictly attend the brethren upon St John's Day, yearly, for commemorating the said Apostle, our Patron and Tutelar Saint, under penalty of forty shillings Scots."

This seems very extraordinary, as a record of what took place in the beginning of the eighteenth century in Presbyterian Scotland. But all the more does it prove the persistence of old rules, of old customs, and of an existence derived from former centuries. The Freemasons probably did not advert to any imaginable incongruity between their customs and the opinions which probably most of them entertained as Presbyterians. It is, however, more important to observe that the date, 1714, is anterior to the date 1717, so that we have proof from the records of the Brechin Lodge of the existence of Freemasonry in Scotland before the time to which modern theorists have ascribed its invention.

LET us endeavour to trace back the history of Masonry a little further. We now come to the *Steinmetzen* of Germany. Findel's account of them (in his "History of Freemasonry," pp. 42–71) may be accepted as correct with regard to facts, although as to the explanation of these facts, and the inferences to be deduced from them, his opinions must be rejected as the mere result of a preconceived notion, that speculative Freemasonry is altogether of recent origin. He begins by acknowledging that "in comparing the social organisation, customs and doctrines of Freemasonry with those of the mediæval building associations, we find many indications of a historical connection between the two institutions." Here it may be observed that we have a mere gratuitous assumption of *two institutions;* but to this it is sufficient at present merely to advert, whilst what follows may very confidently be regarded as proving these so-called two institutions, of which the "*close historical connection*" is admitted, to have been really one. Nor, indeed, is it easy to see how, if a close historical connection existed, the "two institutions" can be deemed to have been truly distinct.

"We recognise," says Findel, "that the following peculiar usages and customs were common to the fraternity of Freemasons at the present day, and the *Steinmetzen* (stone-cutters) of Germany :—(1.) The classification of their members into Masters, fellow-crafts, and apprentices; (2.) The government of the Society by a certain number of officers; (3.) The exclusion of the uninitiated from their community; (4.) The privileges of a Master's son; (5.) The peculiar requisites or qualifications for membership; (6.) The fraternal equality of all the fellows of the craft; (7.) Their mutual obligations to relieve suffering; (8.) Their peculiar laws, jurisdiction, and form of judicature; (9.) The manner of opening and closing their assemblies;

(10.) The ceremonies of initiation into the fraternity; (11.) The usages at their banquets and table-lodges; (12.) The examination of foreign brethren, &c."

No wonder that, after this enumeration of points of agreement, the learned author should go on to say:—" Taking all these circumstances into consideration, and combining with them the results of historical investigation already arrived at, it has been placed beyond all doubt that the modern society is the direct descendant and successor, in an unbroken line, of the operative fraternity of the middle ages." The wonder is that, in face of these facts, he should still speak of the " two institutions " as distinct and essentially different. Apart from evidence of fact, the probability might well be maintained, that these institutions are essentially the same, and that modern Freemasonry is a mere improvement and development of that mediæval Freemasonry of which it is admitted to be the " direct descendant." And this probability is of no small importance in the consideration of the subject. It affords a *primâ facie* ground of opinion, which very positive evidence would be required to set aside.

Into the history of the *Steinmetzen* of Germany it is impossible here to enter. Findel's account of it is very interesting, and probably he is right in most of his opinions as to dates concerning the formation and extension of the fraternity. It is more to our present purpose to consider the actual organisation and system of the fraternity. The following statement is of special importance, and it is remarkable that the German historian of Freemasonry who makes it, never seems for a moment to advert to its importance, or to perceive that it has any bearing on the question of the identity of modern Freemasonry with the Masonry of the mediæval centuries:—" Stonemasons formed a sort of *confraternitas* together, binding themselves by an oath, to which union, besides the confederates, amateurs were also admitted, if they only consented to enter the brotherhood, and submit to its laws."—*Findel*, p. 59. For what reason, it may be asked, were these amateurs admitted, if the fraternity was a mere operative craft? It seems plain that we have here evidence of the existence of speculative Freemasonry, at least in its germ and rudiments ; and it is not necessary that we should attempt to prove more than this in order to identify our modern Freemasonry with that of the mediæval *Steinmetzen* of Germany. It is admitted, on all hands, that Freemasonry has been improved and developed in progress of time, and that it is capable of indefinite improvement. No one is more ready than I to acknowledge that Ashmole, and after him Desaguliers and Anderson, contributed much to the improvement of the system. The only point here contended for is that they found the system already existing, a system such that it attracted their admiration, and that they devoted themselves to its revival and development.

The customs and symbols of the German *Steinmetzen* very nearly agreed with those in use among modern Freemasons. The initiation of a candidate took place in a very similar manner, and the same rules were enforced as to the qualifications of candidates. They are, in fact, the rules which are familiar to every Freemason as contained in the ancient charges; and that they were acknowledged and acted upon in Germany, as well as in England and Scotland, is no small proof of their high antiquity, and of the essential unity of the system, which has prevailed in all parts of the civilised world since modern civilisation began, with that which has sprung from it, and which still prevails where-ever civilisation has extended.

The decline of the German brotherhood began after the Reformation, when the building of cathedrals and monasteries ceased to be the great employment of the age. It was hastened by the troubles of Germany during the Thirty Years' War. Masonry flourishes in times of peace, as it springs from peace, and is productive of peace ; but civil war is of all things the most unfavourable to its progress. When the history of Germany during the sixteenth and seventeenth centuries is considered, it cannot seem wonderful that at the beginning of the eighteenth century, there was little left in the country of the old system of Masonry, although enough remained to afford a starting-point for the improved system then introduced from England.

At the same time that the Lodges (*Bauhütte*) of the German *Steinmetzen* sprang up in Germany, a similar fraternity of Masons formed Lodges in England. Findel chooses to call them *building corporations;* but this is too evidently a term adapted to the mere purpose of a theory. The English Masons, like their continental brethren, recognised each other by secret signs and tokens ; they levied contributions from their members; they relieved the distressed ; they chose their Masters and Wardens, and they held regular meetings and banquets. "Their Lodges were at sunrise, the Master taking his station in the east, and the brethren forming a half-circle around him. After prayer, each craftsman had his daily work pointed out to him, and received his instructions. At sunset they again assembled after labour, prayer was offered, and their wages paid to them."—*Findel*, pp. 75, 76.

It may here be observed that the Masons of Germany, as well as those of England, were distinguished by their high regard for religion, in accordance with the ancient charges, as in fact we find that the Masons in both countries demanded a profession of religion from candidates, and a conduct consistent with that profession from the members of their Order. They did not, however, demand the highest orthodoxy of the Church. Their system was too free for that; and during the middle ages, a continual protest may be said to have been kept up by the Masons in favour of a liberality which had no other existence in these times. The Masons of Germany, in the days of their most flourishing existence, even protected the members of their Order from persecution, and opposed the Inquisition with success.

"In 1389," says Findel, giving a history of the legislative enactments of England respecting Masonry, "it was enacted that, in case of resistance, the Justices of the Peace might call in the assistance of the Sheriff of the county, or the Mayor of the city, or the Alder-

man of the town; they must, therefore, have been present at their
quarterly meetings. The most ancient constitution of 1427, and
Anderson, following its lead, attempt to turn this circumstance into
an honour for the fraternity, leading us to suppose that these
various officers were present in the capacity of initiated brethren.
But we cannot believe that, at that period, amateurs could have
been present as accepted Masons, or as honorary members. Now
and then, possibly, those patrons who were nominated by the King
to superintend the erection of buildings might have been present
at a meeting, but they had certainly no knowledge of the secret
customs and usages of the craft."—*Findel*, p. 77.

It is easy to say, "we cannot believe that at that period
amateurs could have been present," and so on; but all this
is evidently the mere assertion of a preconceived opinion,—
a foregone conclusion. We have made up our mind that there
was nothing in Masonry, during mediæval times, or indeed
till the eighteenth century, but mere operative masonry;
and, therefore, there could be no amateurs accepted as
members of the Lodges!—and so let the world take this
for argument, and adopt our opinion!—Let the sentence
already quoted from Findel, concerning the admission of
amateurs in the Lodges of the *Steinmetzen* of Germany, be
for a moment considered, and the confidence with which he
declares his opinion of the impossibility that amateurs could
be present as accepted Masons, or as as honorary members,
in England, in the fourteenth century, must seem almost
ridiculous. In like manner, his declaration that "now and
then, possibly, those patrons who were nominated by the
King to superintend the erection of buildings might have
been present at a meeting, but they had certainly no knowledge of the secret customs and usages of the craft," must
be set aside as mere gratuitous assertion,—the expression of
an opinion for which no foundation is shown. Nay, in
this assertion it is implied that the patrons nominated
by the King were merely nominated to superintend the
erection of particular buildings,—of which we are far from
having any proof. There might be some difficulty in showing what was really the fact in England; but we have, in

the appointment of the Earl of Orkney and Caithness by James II. of Scotland, proof that something more than the superintendence of the erection of particular buildings was contemplated in royal grants of the same kind in Scotland, and the probability surely is that the state of the case was the same in the two countries. Until plain proof to the contrary is adduced, it must be held that the royally appointed patrons of the Masons of England held an important relation to the whole fraternity, and not merely to those engaged in the erection of particular buildings. On this point, however, further evidence is much to be desired. The probability appears very great on the one side, but it remains for us to hear what can be said, if anything, on the other.

WE may now go still farther back. We partly lose ourselves in the mists of antiquity, and we cannot expect to be able to trace out so intimate a connection between the Masonry of the ancient Romans and that of the present time, as between mediæval and modern Masonry. Yet we find in them such points of agreement as may, at least, nearly be held to identify them as of one system, progressive in its development. and continually changing, whilst yet essentially the same.

The ancient Romans had their architectural colleges (*collegia*), which enjoyed a constitution of their own, and were recognised by the state as a legal body. They were placed under a magistrate, an *ædile* of their own; and in the time of Augustus the members were required to be well skilled, and to have a liberal education. The members of the colleges heard the reports of their officers; and after deliberation, questions were put to the vote, and decided by a majority of votes. " The custom which prevailed among the operatives of the middle ages we find likewise here," says Findel, " viz., that besides the legitimate members of the corporations, lay or amateur members (patrons) were admitted."—*Findel*, p. 22. To this statement it is only necessary to call attention in passing, but its importance in reference to the whole question now under discussion is evidently very great. Nothing can more strongly militate against the opinion that Masonry in the middle ages was a mere operative craft, and that speculative Masonry had then no existence. It carries us back even to the days of the ancient Romans, and gives probability to the opinion that speculative, as well as operative Masonry existed when the Roman colleges flourished in the time of the Roman Republic, and in the most glorious

times of the Roman Empire. " The corporations held their
meetings in secluded rooms, or buildings appropriated
exclusively to that purpose; and most of them had their
own schools for the instruction of apprentices and the lower
grades of workmen.   They had also their own peculiar
religious ceremonies and priests; also an exchequer belong-
ing to the corporation, an archive, and their own seals.
The members took an oath mutually to assist each other;
indigent members received relief, and on their demise were
buried at the expense of the corporation.   They kept regis-
ters of the members, similar to the lists or directories of the
Lodges, some of which are still extant.   They had also their
records, their Masters (*magistri*), Wardens (*decuriones*),
fellow-crafts and apprentices, censors, treasurers, keepers
of archives (*tabularii*), secretaries (*scribæ*), and serving
brethren; their tools and working implements had besides
a symbolical meaning; and in religious matters they were
tolerant."—*Findel*, p. 22.   It is impossible to read this
without perceiving such a strong resemblance to our modern
Freemasonry, that it can hardly be conceived to be acci-
dental, or that the one system did not grow out of the other;
so that in fact it should be deemed the same system developed anew under different circumstances, and with changes
corresponding to the changes of customs and of religion.
Findel notes particularly that a member of the Roman colleges was called *collega*, *incorporatus*, or *collegiatus*, " the
name 'brother' not becoming general till the Christian
masonic fraternity adopted it."   There is nothing in this,
however, to cast doubt on the essential identity of ancient
Roman Masonry with that of our own day.   The idea of
brotherhood amongst men is, indeed, essentially a Christian
one, and its introduction among Masons may probably be
ascribed to the influence of Christianity, although in the
system of the Roman colleges we see more than we could
expect of those sentiments of kindness and acknowledged
equality which it is fitted to indicate.   The attachment of a
symbolical meaning to the tools and working implements
may be safely regarded as one of the first rudiments of

speculative Masonry. " On the tombs of the Roman Masons are to be found not only the compasses, square, plummet, trowel, and hammer, but often two shoes, upon which lie a half-open pair of compasses, perhaps the symbol of a well-spent life, or of conjugal fidelity."

That Roman architectural colleges existed throughout the whole Roman Empire is indisputable. An inscription was found at Chichester in 1725, stating that a college of Masons had erected a temple to Neptune and Minerva. But although Findel admits that a certain connection existed between these Roman colleges and the " building corporations" of later date, he refuses to acknowledge that the latter were a direct continuation of the former, or that the fraternity of Masons can be traced back to the corporations of Rome. " Both these questions," he says, " must be answered in the negative" (the questions may well be deemed almost identical) ; " for the German fraternity of *Steinmetzen* (stone-cutters) have so completely and designedly· metamorphosed the original signification of whatever they, by any possible chance, can have received in a traditional form from the Roman architectural colleges, that we must regard their laws and customs as something essentially new, and totally different from those in use in ancient times."—*Findel*, pp. 23, 24. The force of the reasoning here is not easily to be perceived. That important changes took place may be admitted, but that they were made on purpose, and without regard to the changes of external circumstances, is not to be taken for granted. And even if they were, the fact of the historical connection would remain unaffected. It is only necessary, however, to refer again to the points of agreement in the system of the Roman colleges and that of the German, English, and Scottish masonic Lodges of the middle ages, to see that the relation of the later system to the older must have been that of direct descent. When we see that a child has a strong resemblance to his reputed father, we are naturally inclined to believe in the parentage.

I have quoted from Findel partly from convenience, and

partly because his views on what relates to the 1717 theory
are very opposite to mine. His statements, therefore, cannot be regarded as unfairly adduced by me when adduced
in support of the views which I maintain. Yet I think it
proper to mention that all that is to be found in his work
regarding the Roman *collegia*, had been previously stated
in the written records of Lodges which existed long before
he was born. The fact of their existence at such early
dates is in accordance with my belief as to the antiquity
of Freemasonry,—and leads to the conclusion that the
Freemasons of the present day are the true representatives
of the members of the ancient Roman *collegia*, which
existed before the Christian era.

IF we find reason to think that the present system of Masonry derives its origin from the German *Steinmetzen* of the middle ages, and the similar societies which existed in other countries, and that these also sprang from the architectural colleges of the Romans, we shall have no difficulty in tracing the origin of Freemasonry to a very early age. It is not necessary to follow those authors who have endeavoured to connect Freemasonry, as to its origin, with the building of lyceums and the mysteries of Greece and Egypt. We lose our way here, in the midst of antiquarian lore exceedingly difficult of comprehension. Brother J. Snauberg has endeavoured to demonstrate the connection of Freemasonry with these ancient Greek and Egyptian systems, as well as with the architectural colleges of the Romans. But Findel speaks of the result of his labours with contempt, saying that he has only " proved that schools of architecture and societies of architects existed among the ancients, that the science of architecture is of very ancient date ; and has been transmitted to modern times, and that a similarity is to be found between a few masonic symbols, theories, and customs, and the mysteries of the ancients, the Druids, and the Cimbric bards in Wales, as well as in German legends and fables." Is this, however, of little importance, even if this were all? It would go far to establish a theory of the very ancient origin of Freemasonry, or at least to give probability to such a theory. But we have much more than this in the facts acknowledged by Findel himself; and if we cannot accurately trace the connection of Freemasonry with any ancient Greek or Egyptian system, we may refer with confidence to the general similarity, and hold it probable not

only that the masonic system of the middle ages derived
its origin from that of the ancient Romans, but that the
Roman system also was imported from Greece, into which
country it had come from Egypt, or from some of the most
anciently civilised countries of the East, as the other arts
and sciences, and the very alphabet itself, were derived by
the Greeks from these parts of the world.   Thus we are
brought back to the country in which the Pyramids
were erected and to the times of their erection; and the
probability seems great that there has been a continued
succession of masonic Lodges, colleges, or whatever they
may be called, from that day to this; with many a change,
no doubt, in some of their characters, but yet with an
essential identity of nature and purpose.   This supposition
is made probable by the very nature of Masonry itself, the
acquirements in science necessary for the prosecution of the
art, and the importance of the art in relation to the highest
interests of life, its connection with all the greatness of the
noble and wealthy, and its connection with the religions of
all times and countries.   Whatever the system of religion
was at any time, it had its temples or its churches in all
civilised, or even partially civilised countries; and these
required the utmost efforts of masonic art, even more than
palaces and castles.   The most admirable monuments of
the Masonry of the middle ages are the churches and
cathedrals which exist in all countries of Europe; whilst
if we refer to more ancient times, it is rather to temples
that we look as the great remains of antiquity than to
buildings of any other kind.

The purpose for which the present pamphlet is designed
is merely to show that the theory which ascribes the origin
of modern Freemasonry to the year 1717 is untenable.
This, it is hoped, has been accomplished—first, by evidence of the existence of a system essentially the same
in the seventeenth century; and, secondly, by evidence of
antiquity much beyond this.   Into the latter part of the
subject we have entered only a very little, as it was not
necessary to do more in order to maintain the argument

ntended. Enough, however, has been said to show the high probability of a very ancient origin of Freemasonry, and of the existence of a system in very ancient times essentially the same with that which exists at the present day. Enough has certainly been said to warrant the assertion that the 1717 theory is exploded.

PRINTED BY THE NEW TEMPLE PRESS, 17 GRANT ROAD, CROYDON.

BOOKS PUBLISHED BY
WILLIAM REEVES,
83 Charing Cross Road, London, W.C.

FOLK-LORE OF THE BASUTOS.

BASUTOLAND: ITS LEGENDS AND CUSTOMS. By M. MARTIN. Crown 8vo, cloth, 3s. 6d. *net.* 1903

ENGLISH PROVERBS AND PROVERBIAL PHRASES. By W. CAREW HAZLITT. Collected from the most Authentic Sources, Alphabetically Arranged with Extensive and Valuable Explanatory Notes, together with many References to their Earliest Occurrence. Nearly 600 pages. Thick crown 8vo, cloth, gilt top, 7s. 6d.

POPULAR ANTIQUITIES OF GREAT BRITAIN.

FAITHS AND FOLK-LORE. A Dictionary of National Beliefs, Superstitions, and Popular Customs, Past and Current, with their Classical and Foreign Analogues, Described and Illustrated. Forming a New Edition of "The Popular Antiquities of Great Britain," by BRAND and ELLIS, largely Extended, Corrected and brought down to the Present Time, and now First Alphabetically Arranged. By W. CAREW HAZLITT. Specimens of Reference Headings: Abbot of Bon Accord, Abbot of Unreason, Abingdon, Berks, Abraham-Men, Admiral of the Blue, Adoption, Adventurer, Advertisements and Bills, Æpiornis or Epiornis, Aërolites, Ætites, Afternoon Music, St. Agatha's Letters, St. Agnes Day or Eve, Agues, St. Aldgate, Ale, Ale-house, Ale-Stake or Bush, All Fours, Allhallow Even, All-Hallows, All-Hid, All in the Well, All Saints, Alsatia, Altar, Ambassador, St. Ampoule, Amulets, Anagram, Ancients, St. Andrew's Day, St. Andrew's Well, Aneling, Angelica, Angels or Genii, St. Anne's Well, near Nottingham, St. Anthony of Egypt or Thebes, St. Anthony of Padua, Apostle Spoons, Apparitions, Apple-Howling, Appleton-Thorn, St. Appollonia's Day, etc., etc. 2 vols., 8vo, bevelled cloth, gilt tops, 21s.

LETTERS WRITTEN BY LORD CHESTERFIELD TO HIS SON. Edited, with occasional Elucidatory Notes. Translations of all the Latin, French and Italian Quotations and a Biographical Notice of the Author. By CHARLES STOKES CAREY. With Portrait. Two thick volumes, over 800 pages, cloth.

ARMS AND ARMOUR IN ANTIQUITY AND THE MIDDLE AGES; also a Descriptive Notice of Modern Weapons. By CHARLES BOUTELL. Translated from the French of M. P. LACOMBE. With a Preface, Notes, and an Additional Chapter on Arms and Armour in England. A New Edition. With numerous added Illustrations of fine Specimens from the Collections of Sir Noël Paton, Lord Zouche, Windsor Castle, etc., etc. Crown 8vo, cloth. Published at 7s. 6d.

ENGLISH HERALDRY. Specially Prepared for the Use of Students. By CHARLES BOUTELL. Tenth Edition, Edited and Revised with Additions (including the New Orders recently created) by A. C. Fox-DAVIES. Nearly 500 Illustrations, 367 pages. Crown 8vo, cloth. Published at 7s. 6d.

BOOKS PUBLISHED BY
WILLIAM REEVES,
83 Charing Cross Road, London, W.C.

FREEMASONRY; An Account of the Early History of Free-masonry in England, with Illustrations of the Principles and Precepts advocated by that Institution. By T. L. Fox. 62 pages, post 8vo, cloth, 2s.

THE WAISTCOAT POCKET EDITION.

THE HANDBOOK OF INSTRUCTION IN CRAFT MASONRY. Containing the Entered Apprentice, Fellow-Craft and Master Mason's degrees. By "A Member of the Craft." With Folding Plates of the Three Tracing Boards. 12mo, leather, 4s. *net.*

THE APOCRYPHAL NEW TESTAMENT. Being all the Gospels, Epistles and other pieces now extant attributed in the first four centuries to Jesus Christ, His Apostles and their Companions and not included in the New Testament by its Compilers. By WILLIAM HONE. 8vo, cloth, 3s. 6d.

ANCIENT MYSTERIES DESCRIBED. Especially the English Miracle Plays founded on the Apocryphal New Testament Story, extant among the unpublished MSS. in the British Museum, including notices of Ecclesiastical Shows and Festivals of Fools and Asses, the English Boy Bishop, Descent into Hell, the Lord Mayor's Show, the Guildhall Giants, Christmas Carols, etc. By WILLIAM HONE. With engravings on copper and wood, and index, 300 pages. 8vo, cloth, 3s. 6d.

FLAGELLATION AND THE FLAGELLANTS. A History of the Rod in all Countries from the Earliest Period to the Present Time. By REV. W. COOPER. Twenty plates and other cuts. Very thick crown 8vo, cloth, 7s. 6d.

THE CELEBRATED WORK BY CHEIRO (LEIGH, COUNT DE HAMONG).

CHEIRO'S LANGUAGE OF THE HAND. A Complete Practical Work on the Sciences of Cheirognomy and Cheiromancy. Containing the Systems, Rules and Experience of Cheiro. With Fifty-five Full-page Illustrations and over Two Hundred Engravings of Lines, Mounts and Marks, Drawings of the Seven Types of Theo Doré, etc. Fourteenth Edition, containing Illustrations of the Wonderful Scientific Invention, the Apparatus for "Thought Photography and Register of Cerebral Force." Thick 4to, designed cloth, gilt top, a handsome volume, 10s. 6d. *net.*   1910

"THE KEYSTONE OF ALL THE OCCULT SCIENCES."

ANIMAL MAGNETISM OR MESMERISM AND ITS PHENOMENA. By the late WILLIAM GREGORY, M.D., F.R.S.E. Fifth Edition. With Introduction by "M.A. Oxon." Over 250 pages, 8vo, cloth. Published at 6s. *net.*

PRACTICAL ASTROLOGY. By ALAN LEO. Being a Simple Method of Instruction in the Science of Astrology. New and Revised Edition, with Numerous Diagrams and Tables. Thick Crown 8vo, cloth. Published at 5s. *net.*

Trieste

Trieste Publishing has a massive catalogue of classic book titles. Our aim is to provide readers with the highest quality reproductions of fiction and non-fiction literature that has stood the test of time. The many thousands of books in our collection have been sourced from libraries and private collections around the world.

The titles that Trieste Publishing has chosen to be part of the collection have been scanned to simulate the original. Our readers see the books the same way that their first readers did decades or a hundred or more years ago. Books from that period are often spoiled by imperfections that did not exist in the original. Imperfections could be in the form of blurred text, photographs, or missing pages. It is highly unlikely that this would occur with one of our books. Our extensive quality control ensures that the readers of Trieste Publishing's books will be delighted with their purchase. Our staff has thoroughly reviewed every page of all the books in the collection, repairing, or if necessary, rejecting titles that are not of the highest quality. This process ensures that the reader of one of Trieste Publishing's titles receives a volume that faithfully reproduces the original, and to the maximum degree possible, gives them the experience of owning the original work.

We pride ourselves on not only creating a pathway to an extensive reservoir of books of the finest quality, but also providing value to every one of our readers. Generally, Trieste books are purchased singly - on demand, however they may also be purchased in bulk. Readers interested in bulk purchases are invited to contact us directly to enquire about our tailored bulk rates. Email: customerservice@triestepublishing.com

You May Also Like

The Scottish Church and Its Surroundings, in Early Times

Robert Paton

ISBN: 9780649699247
Paperback: 188 pages
Dimensions: 6.14 x 0.40 x 9.21 inches
Language: eng

The Hamnet Shakspere: Part V. The Winter's Tale: According to the First Folio (Spelling Modernised), with Introduction and Relative Lists

Allan Park Paton

ISBN: 9780649487172
Paperback: 166 pages
Dimensions: 6.14 x 0.35 x 9.21 inches
Language: eng

You May Also Like

ISBN: 9780649248919
Paperback: 58 pages
Dimensions: 6.14 x 0.12 x 9.21 inches
Language: eng

Poetical Pieces, Sacred and Secular: In which are Included Several Poems Specially Designed for Children

A. B. Paton

ISBN: 9780649562558
Paperback: 238 pages
Dimensions: 6.14 x 0.50 x 9.21 inches
Language: eng

Digest of Legal Opinions of Thomas B. Paton, General Counsel of the American Bankers Association, which Have Been Published in the issues of the Journal of the American Bankers Association from July, 1908, to June, 1919, Inclusive

American Bankers Association & T. B. Paton

You May Also Like

A Hand-Book of Benares

Arthur Parker

ISBN: 9780649432882
Paperback: 102 pages
Dimensions: 6.14 x 0.21 x 9.21 inches
Language: eng

A Hand-Book of Scripture Harmony

Anonymous

ISBN: 9780649422647
Paperback: 106 pages
Dimensions: 5.5 x 0.22 x 8.25 inches
Language: eng

You May Also Like

Aids to a holy life, in forms for self-examination, general and particular, compiled from various sources with introduction, explaining the manner in which the duty should be performed

Thomas H. B. Bund

ISBN: 9780649346844
Paperback: 86 pages
Dimensions: 5.25 x 0.18 x 8.0 inches
Language: eng

A lecture on science and revelation

James Stuart

ISBN: 9780649262847
Paperback: 52 pages
Dimensions: 6.14 x 0.11 x 9.21 inches
Language: eng

Find more of our titles on our website. We have a selection of thousands of titles that will interest you. Please visit

www.triestepublishing.com

Lightning Source UK Ltd.
Milton Keynes UK
UKHW02f0830070618
323878UK00007B/673/P